S. HRG. 112–706

REGULATION OF TRIBAL GAMING: FROM BRICK AND MORTAR TO THE INTERNET

HEARING

BEFORE THE

COMMITTEE ON INDIAN AFFAIRS
UNITED STATES SENATE

ONE HUNDRED TWELFTH CONGRESS

SECOND SESSION

JULY 26, 2012

Printed for the use of the Committee on Indian Affairs

U.S. GOVERNMENT PRINTING OFFICE

78–446 PDF   WASHINGTON : 2013

For sale by the Superintendent of Documents, U.S. Government Printing Office
Internet: bookstore.gpo.gov   Phone: toll free (866) 512–1800; DC area (202) 512–1800
Fax: (202) 512–2104   Mail: Stop IDCC, Washington, DC 20402–0001

CONTENTS

WITNESSES

APPENDIX

REGULATION OF TRIBAL GAMING: FROM BRICK AND MORTAR TO THE INTERNET

THURSDAY, JULY 26, 2012

U.S. SENATE,
COMMITTEE ON INDIAN AFFAIRS,
Washington, DC.

The Committee met, pursuant to notice, at 2:30 p.m. in room 628, Dirksen Senate Office Building, Hon. Daniel K. Akaka, Chairman of the Committee, presiding.

OPENING STATEMENT OF HON. DANIEL K. AKAKA, U.S. SENATOR FROM HAWAII

The CHAIRMAN. I call this hearing on the Committee of Indian Affairs to order.

Aloha and welcome to all of you here. Welcome to the Committee's oversight hearing on the Regulation of Tribal Gaming: From Brick and Mortar to the Internet.

Today we are here to discuss the regulation of Tribal gaming. Tribal gaming is now a $27 billion industry. In total, the Tribal gaming makes up approximately 40 percent of the commercial gaming industry in the United States. Gaming, like many industries, does not remain stagnant. That is why today we will discuss the current regulatory structure of Indian gaming under the Indian Gaming Regulatory Act, as well as examine regulation of online gaming should Federal legislation be enacted.

Gaming has been the single most effective of economic development for Indian Country. Revenues from gaming provide essential services to Tribal members, including education, health care, and housing. Indian gaming also provides jobs to members of the surrounding communities. In many counties across the Nation, Tribes are the largest employer, with nearly 75 percent of those jobs going to non-Indians.

With these types of economic tools comes great responsibility. Tribes are the first line regulators for Tribal gaming. We, in Congress, and especially on this Committee, also have a responsibility to ensure that Tribal views and priorities are part of any legislation that could impact Tribal gaming.

That is why I have developed a draft online gaming bill, the Tribal Online Gaming Act of 2012. This bill is intended to further the dialogue with Tribes, my colleagues here in the Senate, and other affected stakeholders as well. I encourage all of you to review the bill and provide any comments.

In any expansion of gaming we must make sure that the unique circumstances surrounding Tribal sovereignty are maintained in any legislation and we must also enable Tribes to participate fully, should any legislation be considered, so Tribes are on equal footing with their counterparts in the commercial gaming industry.

I look forward to hearing from all of our witnesses on how we can ensure that Tribal gaming is properly regulated and it exists now and into the future.

Today we have the Chair of the NIGC, who will update the Committee on that agency's regulatory efforts over the years. We also have Tribal leaders from the Mohegan and Tulalip Tribes. Both these gentlemen have testified on the online gaming issue in the past and will update us on their Tribe's activities on this issue.

Finally, we will hear from experts in the field of gaming. I am sure all of you will provide valuable insights today.

Let me now call on our Vice Chairman, Senator Barrasso, for his opening statement.

STATEMENT OF HON. JOHN BARRASSO, U.S. SENATOR FROM WYOMING

Senator BARRASSO. Mr. Chairman, thank you very much for holding this hearing.

Last November, this Committee held an oversight hearing on the future of Internet gaming in Indian Country. Early this year we held an oversight hearing on the Department of Justice's opinion regarding Internet gaming and its implications for Indian Country.

While there are many unanswered questions regarding Internet gaming in the United States, one thing is clear: the regulation of Internet gaming must be sufficient and effective. We are going to hear today how Tribes are preparing for such regulation. We will also hear from the National Indian Gaming Commission about developments since our hearing about a year ago.

As you mentioned, Mr. Chairman, according to the Commission, gross revenues for Indian gaming in 2011 were over $27 billion and, as you said, that is a significant amount of money. Again, though, as we discussed a year ago, the annual compliance reports do not effectively assess how theft and crime at gaming facilities are being addressed. So I am looking forward to hearing what, if any, progress on this issue and other issues raised last year has been made.

So thank you, Mr. Chairman, for your leadership on this important matter. I look forward to the witnesses' testimony and welcome them here.

The CHAIRMAN. Thank you very much, Senator Barrasso.

Let me now call on Senator Franken for any comments he may have.

STATEMENT OF HON. AL FRANKEN, U.S. SENATOR FROM MINNESOTA

Senator FRANKEN. Thank you, Mr. Chairman.

As we all know, gaming has been an incredibly powerful economic development tool for Tribes. Gaming enterprises have brought much needed revenue and jobs to Indian Country. Tribes have used gaming revenue to become self-sufficient to invest in their communities and to provide basic services its members.

The Mille Lacs Band of Ojibwe in Central Minnesota uses revenue from its two casinos to fund health clinics, an impressive assisted living facility, a police department, wastewater treatment facility, and schools. Mille Lacs is committed to providing affordable, safe, and comfortable housing to all of its members. Since 1991, the Band has built more than 200 new homes and renovated many existing homes. Mille Lacs has also been able to invest in a number of non-gaming businesses and runs a small business development program to support members who want to start their own businesses.

Indian gaming has also had a much broader economic impact. The Shakopee Mdewakanton Sioux Community, southwest of the Twin Cities, about 45 minutes southwest, is a great example of how gaming revenue can transform an entire community. Shakopee employs over 4,000 individuals, both gaming and non-gaming enterprises. They are the largest employer in Scott County, providing one in every ten jobs. In 2011, the Shakopee gaming enterprise was named one of the Minneapolis Star Tribune's top workplaces in the State based on a survey of employees.

Shakopee has also had an impressive charitable giving program. Just over the past four years, the Tribe has donated nearly $128 million. Of that amount, over $115 million went to other Indian Tribes for economic development and community improvements.

Without the revenue and opportunities that Indian gaming provides, none of this would be possible. Gaming is far from a perfect solution. Many Tribes are not able to take advantage of gaming opportunities because of their location, and much more needs to be done to diversify the economies of all Tribes. But gaming has provided an opportunity for so many Tribes. It has strengthened Tribal sovereignty and allowed Tribes to take hold of their own future. It is a tool that, if used well, can make a huge difference. This is something worth protecting.

Any changes, any changes to current gaming laws must take into account the special place that Tribes hold in the gaming industry, both to respect Tribal sovereignty and out of economic fairness. If Congress considers legislation to legalize Internet gaming, it is vitally important that Tribes be consulted at every step of the process.

I want to thank you, Chairman Akaka, for continuing to hold hearings on this important subject. I would like to thank the Vice Chairman as well. I hope we can all work together to make sure that the rights of gaming Tribes are protected. Thank you.

The CHAIRMAN. Thank you very much, Senator Franken.

As Chairman, it is my goal to ensure that we hear from all, all who want to contribute to the discussion. The hearing record is open for two weeks from today and I encourage everyone to submit your comments through written testimony.

I want to remind the witnesses to please limit your oral testimony to 5 minutes today.

So I would like to say Aloha and welcome our first panelists, Ms. Tracie Stevens, Chairwoman of the National Indian Gaming Commission. Would you please proceed with your testimony?

STATEMENT OF HON. TRACIE STEVENS, CHAIRWOMAN, NATIONAL INDIAN GAMING COMMISSION

Ms. STEVENS. Thank you, Chairman Akaka, Vice Chairman Barrasso, and members of the Committee for inviting me to testify today. It is an honor to appear before this Committee as the Chairwoman of the National Indian Gaming Commission. I am a member of the Tulalip Tribes of Washington State.

With me today are Vice Chair Stephanie Cochran and Commissioner Dan Little. Additionally, I would like to recognize members of my own council who are here today, Dawn Hatch and Glen Gobin.

As a Commission, we have established four major priorities: consultation and relationship building, training and technical assistance, regulatory review, and agency operations. Today I will discuss the status of Tribal gaming and provide an update on these four priorities.

Over the past few years, gaming revenue has remained stable, generating approximately $27.2 billion in gross revenue for Tribes. In 2011, 237 Tribes engaged in gaming, with 421 gaming operations.

There are over 6,500 Tribal, State, and Federal regulators working together to maintain the integrity of Indian gaming. NIGC is the Federal civil regulatory agency primarily responsible, along with Tribal and State regulators, for regulation of Indian gaming on Indian lands. Tribal Governments employ approximately 5,900 gaming regulators and States employ approximately 570 regulators. In addition to working with Tribal and State regulators, at the Federal level, NIGC works with Federal agencies such as the Federal Bureau of Investigation, the Department of Interior, and the Department of Treasury and Justice to promote compliance with all Federal laws.

NIGC has worked to successfully implement a regulatory approach we refer to ACE, assistance, compliance, and enforcement, in that order. The approach has effectively reduced the number of notices of violation by proactively addressing potential issues and proceeding with enforcement action only for issues that could not be resolved.

As I have discussed previously, Class III MICS are essential to protect the integrity and security of gaming operations. All Tribes engaged in Class III gaming pursuant to a Tribal-State compact have systems of internal controls that govern procedures for Class III operations.

Although we do not have independent authority to promulgate or enforce Class III MICS, it has always been the practice of the NIGC to work with Tribes to strengthen the effectiveness of their Class III MICS, and we continue that practice today.

Meaningful and transparent Tribal consultation is one of our four priorities. We transformed our consultation process to make it inclusive, meaningful, and transparent. In the past year, we have conducted 19 consultations as part of our regulatory review. Approximately 345 Tribal leaders or their representatives from approximately 179 Tribes attended these consultations.

The Commission also views training and technical assistance as a critical tool in maintaining the integrity of Indian gaming. In

2011, the NIGC provided 83 trainings, totaling 659 training hours. In 2011, over 2300 individuals attended training sessions, and so far this year 1,069 individuals from 132 Tribes have attended trainings.

We have also worked to improve the internal function of the agency by streamlining our internal operations. Tribal revenues are the sole funding source for the NIGC, and it is imperative that NIGC utilize these revenues efficiently and effectively. This means a smarter, better equipped agency that is more responsive and better adapts to its regulatory responsibilities and the needs of the Tribal gaming industry.

Review of our regulations is another critical focus for the agency. We are committed to maintaining a regulatory framework that is efficient and effective. Over the past year, we have examined 20 regulations or potential regulations and circulated 13 discussion drafts. Since July 2011, we have published 10 proposed rules and 2 final rules. The Commission is working diligently to complete these rulemakings.

A focus of our rulemaking is on the Class II MICS and technical standards. These regulations provide minimum standards designed to protect the security and integrity of Class II gaming operations and equipment used to play Class II games. Updating the MICS and technical standards for Class II gaming are integral to protecting the industry and patrons alike.

This concludes my testimony, and I hope this summary of activities and initiatives provides the Committee with valuable information regarding the regulatory role and the goals of the NIGC. Thank you, Chairman Akaka, Vice Chairman Barrasso, and members of the Committee for your time and attention today. I am available to answer any questions that you may have.

[The prepared statement of Ms. Stevens follows:]

PREPARED STATEMENT OF HON. TRACIE STEVENS, CHAIRWOMAN, NATIONAL INDIAN GAMING COMMISSION

Thank you, Chairman Akaka, Vice Chairman Barrasso, and members of the Committee for inviting me to testify today. It is an honor to appear before you in my capacity as Chairwoman for the National Indian Gaming Commission (NIGC or Commission).

During our tenure with the Commission, the Commissioners have established four major priorities: consultation and relationship building; training and technical assistance; regulatory review; and agency operations. We have made significant progress on each of these four priorities since I was sworn into office in June 2010. Meaningful consultation and relationship building are paramount in maintaining strong regulation of the industry by Federal, tribal and state regulators. NIGC-sponsored training opportunities and technical assistance provide early resources to address potential regulatory issues, thereby maintaining the integrity of Indian gaming. Regulatory review improves the industry by establishing clear, effective standards. Finally, review of our internal operations promotes efficient and effective regulation by eliminating redundancies, work silos, and unnecessary processes.

Each of the four priorities aids NIGC's administration of its statutory responsibilities as set forth in the Indian Gaming Regulatory Act (IGRA). As I have discussed in prior testimony, this Commission has established the "ACE" approach to enforcement consistent with the four priorities: assistance, compliance, and enforcement. This approach prevents foreseeable problems through effective communication, training and technical assistance, and compliance efforts. When necessary, the Commission takes enforcement action to ensure compliance and protect the integrity of Indian gaming.

Today I will discuss the status of tribal gaming and provide an update on the Commission's progress in achieving its four priorities.

The Current Status of Indian Gaming and Regulatory Oversight

Gaming revenue provides resources for many tribal services as well as thousands of jobs for tribal members and surrounding communities. Currently, gaming operations employ tens of thousands of individuals across the United States, mostly in areas that, historically, suffer from high unemployment. Over the past few years, gaming revenue has remained roughly stable, collectively generating approximately $27.2 billion in gross revenue for tribes. In 2011, 237 tribes engaged in gaming as a means of tribal economic development, with 421 active gaming operations.

There are over 6,500 tribal, state, and Federal regulators working together to maintain the integrity of Indian gaming. NIGC is the Federal civil regulatory agency primarily responsible—along with tribal and state regulators—for regulation of Indian gaming on Indian lands. Tribal governments employ approximately 5,900 gaming regulators and states employ approximately 570 regulators. In addition to working with tribal and state regulators, at the Federal level, NIGC works with Federal agencies such as the Federal Bureau of Investigation, the Department of the Interior, the Department of Treasury and the Department of Justice, to promote compliance with all Federal laws.

During the last 12 months, the NIGC has successfully implemented the ACE approach. In addition to providing informal day-to-day technical assistance, our auditors, compliance officers and attorneys work closely with tribes to resolve compliance issues in a manner that takes into account unique aspects of a particular gaming operation. If compliance steps are unsuccessful, we take enforcement action. ACE has effectively reduced the number of notices of violations (NOVs) by proactively addressing potential compliance issues and proceeding with enforcement action only for substantial regulatory violations that were not, or could not, be corrected through technical assistance and compliance efforts.

As the Committee is aware, six years ago the D.C. Circuit held that the NIGC does not possess authority to promulgate regulations establishing Minimum Internal Controls (MICS) for Class III gaming. As I have discussed in my previous testimony, Class III MICS are essential to protect the integrity and security of gaming operations. During my tenure as Chairwoman, we have examined the real world impact of the court's decision on the regulation of Indian gaming.

Through research and working with tribes and tribal regulators, we have learned that all tribes engaged in Class III gaming pursuant to a tribal-state compact have Class III MICS. Of the 24 states that allow Class III gaming, 15 require stringent MICS specifically in their compacts, and the other nine states require tribes to develop comprehensive MICS of their own. Therefore, every such tribe has a system of internal controls that governs procedures for Class III operations.

The Commission has never taken an enforcement action for failure to comply with MICS. Prior to the decision in *Colorado River Indian Tribes v. National Indian Gaming Commission,* 466 F.3d 134 (D.C. Cir. 2006), (CRIT) if NIGC identified an issue with a particular tribe's Class III MICS, the agency worked with the tribe to achieve compliance. Although we do not have independent authority to promulgate or enforce Class III MICS, tribes continue to request our assistance and we continue to work with them to strengthen the effectiveness of their Class III MICS.

We have also consulted with tribes regarding how the Commission should address the D.C. Circuit's decision. While there does not appear to be a tribal consensus, many tribes support publication of Class III MICS as guidance for their own regulations and compacts. We continue to utilize the MICS to provide technical assistance and training, and many tribes utilize NIGC's Class III MICS as part of their own regulatory schemes or as part of their tribal-state compacts.

Consultation and Relationship Building

Meaningful and transparent consultation with tribes is integral to the success of NIGC's mission. As the primary Federal civil regulatory agency, the Commission conducts government-to-government consultations regarding changes to its regulations. This government-to-government dialogue is crucial in maintaining the integrity of the industry given the tribal, state and federal regulatory roles under IGRA.

We make every effort to consult throughout Indian country and bring NIGC to tribal communities and widely-attended gatherings, in an effort to be mindful of both tribal and NIGC resources. In the past 12 months, we have conducted 19 consultations in every region of the United States regarding regulatory review. Tribal leaders and representatives from approximately 179 tribes attended, totaling approximately 345 individuals.

We have also been working collaboratively with Federal, tribal and state officials to ensure roles under IGRA are coordinated. This promotes effective inter-governmental communications regarding gaming issues and helps ensure that the appropriate agency has the information and support needed to perform its duties. As such, the Commission has reached out to the Federal Bureau of Investigation, the Department of Justice, Financial Crimes Enforcement Network, and other agencies, to develop inter-agency practices and to participate in inter-agency work groups.

Technical Assistance and Training

The Commission views training and technical assistance as a critical tool in bolstering industry security and maintaining compliance with regulatory and statutory requirements. Therefore, consistent with express mandates contained in IGRA and the goals of the Commission, the NIGC offers training and technical assistance to tribal governments, tribal regulators and gaming operations personnel. Successful regulation depends on a well-trained workforce and well-targeted training to ensure compliance with Federal regulations. Our goal is to achieve compliance with IGRA before issues arise, which will serve to preserve the integrity of tribal gaming and preempt the need for enforcement actions.

Last year, we conducted a survey of our program, which helped inform our review and revisions to our course catalog. As a result, requests for training and technical assistance, as well as participation in trainings, have risen.

In 2011, the NIGC provided 83 training programs, totaling 659 training hours. Over 2,300 individuals attended training sessions, representing 209 (87 percent) of all gaming tribes. So far this year, 1069 individuals from 132 tribes have attended our training programs. The NIGC has offered 51 different types of training. As more tribes learn about training opportunities, we expect trainings and attendance to continue to increase.

Training and technical assistance will be an on-going initiative in our mission to achieve full compliance and serve the needs of the industry.

Internal Agency Operations

As part of our effort to optimize regulation of tribal gaming, we have removed work flow silos, eliminated redundant functions, streamlined and implemented better processes to improve the functioning of the Agency. Further, in accordance with requirements of the Government Performance and Results Modernization Act of 2010, P.L. 111–352, we are in the process of drafting a strategic plan, which will outline the NIGC's priorities over the next several years. The plan also will detail processes and methods by which the NIGC will achieve its goals, including performance measurements to assess the success of each initiative. In addition, consistent with Executive Order 13589, ''Promoting Efficient Spending,'' we are continuously examining how to promote the cost-effective use of resources, including the hiring of staff to build upon NIGC's capabilities to perform mission-critical functions efficiently.

To maximize efficiency within the Agency, we have adopted or revised internal policies to provide clarity to our employees. We are fully utilizing existing contracts with other agencies, which are cost effective. Tribal revenues are the sole funding source for the NIGC, and it is imperative that NIGC utilize these revenues efficiently and effectively. This means a smarter, better-equipped Agency that is more responsive and better adapts to its regulatory responsibilities and needs of the tribal gaming industry.

In addition to its efforts to increase internal efficiency, the NIGC has continued its commitment to transparency by holding public meetings on the state of the Agency and important issues. Our most recent public meeting was held on May 23, 2012 in Prior Lake, Minnesota. These meetings provide tribes, as well as the public, an opportunity to learn about Commission business and to address the Commission. We will continue to hold public meetings to inform the community of the NIGC's progress toward achievement of its four priorities and other operational issues.

Regulatory Review

We embarked on this important initiative in November 2010. Review of our regulations focused on maintaining a regulatory framework that is efficient and effective. Through internal deliberation, tribal consultation, and public comment, we are promulgating improvements that streamline processes while maximizing the NIGC's ability to regulate the industry effectively.

After consulting with tribes and considering public comment in response to a Notice of Intent, the Commission established a Regulatory Review priority list and consultation schedule. This initiative has been conducted in accordance with Executive Order 13563, ''Improving Regulations and Regulatory Review,'' issued on Jan 18, 2011. Over the past year, we have discussed 20 regulations or potential regulations, and circulated 13 discussion drafts to date. Since I appeared before you in 2011, the Commission has published 10 Notices of Proposed Rule, two Notices of No Action and two Final Rules. Of the 10 Notices of Proposed Rule, the Commission is working diligently to conclude those rulemakings by issuing final rules in the Federal Register.

This Commission is dedicated to strong and efficient regulation of Indian gaming. Therefore, a large portion of our effort has been focused on reviewing and updating the Class II Minimum Internal Control Standards (MICS) and Technical Standards for Gaming Equipment Used With the Play of Class II Games, 25 C.F.R. Parts 543 and 547. These regulations outline minimum standards designed to protect the security and integrity of Class II gaming operations, as well as minimum standards for equipment used to play Class II games. Through internal deliberations and consultation with tribes, we are reviewing the current regulations to ensure that they provide for advances in technology and continue to be relevant to current state of the industry. Updating the MICS and Technical Standards for Class II gaming are integral to protecting the industry and patrons alike.

As part of the review process for Parts 543 and 547, we developed a Tribal Advisory Committee (TAC) to advise and make recommendations to the Commission regarding the Class II MICS and Technical Standards. The TAC is comprised of diverse group of tribal government representatives whose expertise assisted the Commission in its review of Parts 543 and 547, and aided in the development of a discussion draft, which was published on March 16, 2012.

We consulted with tribes in nearly all regions of the United States and reviewed over 50 written public comments to the discussion drafts. Although many tribes expressed opposition to potential changes to current regulations, the Commission's regulatory role is to take a hard look at the issues and make well informed decisions, even if those decisions ultimately are unpopular with the regulated community. The Commission is dedicated to promulgating strong regulations that maintain the integrity of Indian gaming.

The Commission's proposed rules, which were published on June 1, 2012, are based on careful consideration of comments received on discussion drafts. Since the proposed rules were published, we have conducted five consultations in various regions of the country and continue to receive written comments. The comment period for the proposed rules will close on August 15, 2012, after which we will review all public comments, allowing the NIGC to make a well informed and fully considered decision regarding final regulations.

Conclusion

This concludes my testimony. I hope this summary of activities and initiatives provides the Committee with valuable information regarding the regulatory role and goals of the NIGC.

Thank you, Chairman Akaka, Vice-Chairman Barrasso, and members of the Committee for your time and attention today. I am available to answer any questions you might have for me.

The CHAIRMAN. Thank you very much.

Now I would like to, before we ask you any questions, I would like to call on Senator Udall for any comments or opening statement he may have.

STATEMENT OF HON. TOM UDALL,
U.S. SENATOR FROM NEW MEXICO

Senator UDALL. Let me just be very brief, because I think we are at the witness stage and I would like to go directly to the witnesses and the questioning here.

First of all, Chairman Akaka, I want to thank you for holding this important hearing on Tribal gaming and for remaining engaged in this issue as the talk of legalized Internet gaming continues. Gaming is an issue with significant impact on Indian Country, and the Committee and Tribal leaders need to be an active part of the debate over any possible legislation relating to gaming in our Nation, and the Tribes need to have a seat at the table.

Beyond this hearing, it is my hope that my colleagues in Congress will engage Tribes in development of any legislative proposals related to gaming, especially in relation to Internet gaming. As

Tribal Nations grapple to develop strong economies and healthy communities, gaming will continue to be a significant factor.

With that, Chairman Akaka, I would yield back and look forward to the questioning period that we are about ready to undergo. Thank you.

The CHAIRMAN. Thank you very much, Senator Udall.

Ms. Stevens, the NIGC's current fee structure allows for a total budget of $18 million per year. Is that amount sufficient for the NIGC to carry out its regulatory function for the 240 Tribes who conduct gaming?

Ms. STEVENS. Thank you, Chairman Akaka, for that question. I believe that the current fee structure is sufficient to fund the NIGC's operations at this time. Also, as I said, in our initiatives we are working to maximize the resources that we have at the agency, and we continue to do so. So based on our current budget forecast, I believe the current structure is sufficient.

The CHAIRMAN. Thank you.

Ms. Stevens, Tribal gaming revenues for 2011 show an increase for the first time since 2008. Given this trend in the industry, do you anticipate that jobs in the industry will also increase?

Ms. STEVENS. Thank you, Chairman. While we don't have that information available to us, I would imagine that higher revenues may result in additional jobs either at Tribal gaming operations or Tribal Governments and their businesses.

The CHAIRMAN. Thank you.

Now let me call on the Vice Chair for any questions he may have. Senator Barrasso.

Senator BARRASSO. Thank you, Mr. Chairman.

As you know, some States have now begun the process of legalizing some forms of online gaming in their jurisdictions, and the role of the Federal Government and Tribal Governments in Internet gaming is being discussed, but it really still remains up in the air for now. What regulatory changes should Congress or Tribes consider if Tribes were able to engage in Internet gaming?

Ms. STEVENS. Thank you, Vice Chairman. Without legislation, I couldn't speak directly to what our regulatory role would be. In terms of what implications the States might consider, or the Federal Government, regarding the Tribes or the opportunities for the Tribes, I would leave that to the Tribes to discuss. As a Federal regulator, we are focused on our position with regulating, and we would be happy to work with the Committee in the future should legislation be dropped.

Senator BARRASSO. Last year you testified that the Commission was examining approaches for ensuring that the minimum internal control standards for Tribal gaming would be implemented, and your testimony now indicates that every Tribe has a system of internal controls. In 9 of the 24 States allowing gaming, Tribes develop their own standards. The question I would have is how does the National Indian Gaming Commission ensure that Tribal minimum internal control standards at all Tribal operations are sufficient to protect the integrity of the games?

Ms. STEVENS. Thank you, Vice Chairman. Just to get some context, Indian gaming takes place in 28 States. In 24 States Tribes participate in Class III gaming pursuant to a Class III gaming compact, which is the agreement between the Tribes and the States, and, as you said, there are 9 that the compact directs the Tribe to have comprehensive MICS.

And what we do, we work with Tribal regulators and operators to provide training and technical assistance but, more importantly, our staff reviews agreed upon procedures, which are audits that are on operations that are performed by independent audit firms, and in those States those audits confirm that each of those States and those Tribes have comprehensive MICS. So we have what we call AUPs, they are called agreed upon procedures. Those are audits by independent firms and they confirm the existence of comprehensive minimal internal control standards.

Senator BARRASSO. Following up on that, your written testimony says that successful regulation depends upon a well trained workforce, and you say several training sessions are offered by your agency. Do you have some way to measure the effectiveness of this training, and could you please explain how you measure that effectiveness?

Ms. STEVENS. Thank you, Vice Chairman. Evaluating effectiveness has multiple layers. We get feedback from Tribal employees and the regulators and operators. We also, more importantly, get feedback from our regional staff. We have seven regional offices and three satellite offices. They are on the ground every day, out working with Tribes, so we get feedback; they do site visits, they also look at these AUPs, and we evaluate compliance reports that we get from our staff when they do these site visits.

As my written testimony says, training is really important; it helps keep Tribes in compliance and it prevents violations. So those are the ways that we measure effectiveness. And something to note, our training requests and the voluntary just general requests that we get from Tribes for help has increased substantially since we started these initiatives.

Senator BARRASSO. Last August, the Committee sent several questions to you from the July 2011 oversight hearing, and I know our Committee clerks' records show that we haven't yet received responses to the questions. I understand that perhaps your staff hadn't submitted the questions to you.

We are likely to submit some more questions to you. I would ask that in two weeks or maybe next week, you actually look to see that you have received the questions and in a very timely way get backto us. I was looking for answers to questions from a year ago and we still don't have those in writing, and there may have been some lost in the communication. But I would ask you to actively look for the questions because they are going to be coming after this hearing, so thank you very much.

Ms. STEVENS. Vice Chairman, I apologize for that. I recall drafting those answers and authorizing them, and at this time it was sort of a surprise to us last night, when we were checking with staff, that you had not received them, and I apologize for that. We will work to get you a copy of that.

Senator BARRASSO. Thank you. Thank you very much.

Thank you, Mr. Chairman

The CHAIRMAN. Thank you very much, Senator Barrasso.

Senator Franken, your questions, please.

Senator FRANKEN. Yes, thank you, Mr. Chairman

Ms. Stevens, you are Chairwoman of the National Indian Gaming Commission. The Commission has almost 25 years of experience regulating Indian gaming. You currently oversee 422 gaming facilities in 28 States.

The legalization of Internet gaming is controversial in and of itself for many reasons. Gaming and Indian gaming is something that, I imagine, if you are like and my job, you think about a good 12, 14 hours a day. So I would just like to ask you what do you are the issues that we should be thinking about when we are talking about the impact on Indian Tribes, on Indian gaming, when we talk about the legalization of Internet gaming? Very general question, obviously.

Ms. STEVENS. Well, thank you, Senator Franken. You know, as a regulatory body, we focus on regulation and what we are currently authorized to regulate, so in the abstract it is difficult to answer that question. I think that, as a Federal regulator, I would defer to the Tribes to talk about that.

Senator FRANKEN. I am not asking necessarily for your opinions about what is good, what is the best way to do things, et cetera, et cetera. Just delineate if you could, as I said, this is something you must think about a lot, you must give thought to. What are the issues that we should be thinking about? What are the areas? I am asking you because you are Chairwoman of the National Indian Gaming Commission. What aspects of this should we be thinking about in terms of the impacts on Indian gaming, in terms of the impact on Indian Tribes?

Ms. STEVENS. Well, again, I think as a regulator, and not necessarily from the Tribal perspective, and I would be interested in what Tribes have to say, but what I do think about is because IGRA has a three-tiered, from a regulatory standpoint, three-tiered regulatory system, there is NIGC, there are the States, and there are the Tribes. In addition to that, because we don't have criminal authority, as I said, we have the Department of Justice, FBI, IRS, Treasury, all these other agencies.

So I would say those are things that I think about. It is sort of the who is on first, who is going to do what? And it is hard for me to give any recommendation about that, but that is what I am thinking about, is the jurisdiction because it is divided up by the Act.

Senator FRANKEN. So what you are thinking most about is the regulatory regime.

Ms. STEVENS. Yes. I wonder what that is going to look like.

Senator FRANKEN. Okay, so that is what you think about 12 to 14 hours a day.

Ms. STEVENS. I am a regulator.

Senator FRANKEN. Okay.

Ms. STEVENS. That is what I do.

Senator FRANKEN. I apologize. That is your job, is regulating, so that is what you think about and that is proper. In your testimony you state that meaningful consultation and relationship building are paramount to maintaining regulation of the industry. Can you elaborate on the importance of consultation for effective regulation and how do you do that?

Ms. STEVENS. Well, thank you, Senator Franken. Because it is a three-tiered system and because Tribes and their regulators are on the ground 24 hours a day, 7 days a week, they are the day-to-day regulators. In addition to that, and more importantly, as has been made clear by the President's memo in November 2009, we take consultation in our government-to-government relationship with Tribes very seriously. Because there are so many different roles for different agencies, for Tribes, States, and Federal bodies, we have to collaborate, and in keeping with the spirit of government-to-government relationship and respecting the spirit of self-determination and sovereignty with Tribes, we have to talk to them, especially with regard to regulations that they will also be implementing.

It is not just NIGC who is making sure that we are in compliance; the Tribes are using these regulations. And in talking to Tribes in this past 18 months about the regulations that we have been reviewing, we have talked to them before we started making changes so that we get a better sense from a practical standpoint how any changes might affect their ability to regulate, their ability to operate.

So it is very important for us to do that, and it also keeps the communication channels open. If a Tribe needs help, if they need technical assistance or training, we want them to come to us; we don't want them to be in fear of us. And the only way we get that is if we have open communications and we are consulting with them.

Senator FRANKEN. My time is up. I probably will submit some questions for you also, so look for those. One is if Internet gaming were legalized tomorrow, which regulators would be overseeing that, but that will be a written question you can look for.

Ms. STEVENS. Thank you, Senator.

Senator FRANKEN. Thank you.

The CHAIRMAN. Thank you very much, Senator Franken.

Senator Udall, your questions.

Senator UDALL. Thank you, Chairman Akaka.

Ms. Stevens, what do you believe are the biggest issues that are facing you as Chairman of the National Indian Gaming Commission? What are the challenges that you are facing in your current regulatory capacity, you and the other commissioners?

Senator UDALL. I am not sure that they are challenges, necessarily, as much as the areas in which we focus, which I explained in my testimony. We want to make sure that Tribes are staying compliant. I think that is what my primary responsibility is and what, as Senator Franken said, I think about 12 to 14 hours a day, and sometimes longer and sometimes in the middle of the night, keeping Tribes in compliance and how do we do that.

Following up on what I was saying to Senator Franken, keeping those communication lines open, because we do have to work with the Tribes. So I wouldn't say necessarily that it is a challenge, but more of a focus of making sure that we are in compliance.

Senator UDALL. How are we doing on compliance, in your judgment and in the judgment of the Commission and the folks that are out there working on compliance?

Ms. STEVENS. As I said, there are a number of ways that we measure the effectiveness of what we do, and I think we are doing fairly well. Tribes are coming to us when they have issues, when they need technical assistance and training. We have audit staff on the ground who are always willing to help. We are working with Tribes on regulations to make sure that the regulations are relevant for today and to provide Tribal regulators with the tools they need to regulate.

Senator UDALL. What are the measures you use on compliance? You mentioned a couple of measures that you look at.

Ms. STEVENS. Well, as I said, we have what we call AUPs, which are the agreed upon procedure audits. Every year the Tribes are required to submit their financial statements to us. Those are indicators. We also, like I said, we have site visits, and those site visits provide us with compliance reports, and we act accordingly with regard to any issues that come up with those visits.

Senator UDALL. What percentage of Tribes are out of compliance on the AUPs or in the other measures that you use?

Ms. STEVENS. I would have to check with our staff to see exactly what that number is, and we would be happy to report back to you.

Senator UDALL. That would be great, if you could submit that for the record.

What do you see as the future of Tribal gaming? Do you expect an expansion of Tribal gaming or do you expect it to stay about where it is right now?

Ms. STEVENS. Well, again, as a regulator, I concern myself primarily with regulating. However it might expand, whether by more facilities or more Tribes partaking in what is currently authorized, or if Congress authorizes additional opportunities, we will follow through with what Congress enacts.

Senator UDALL. And then this question goes to that. You know, I know this is a big if and you are trying to not get into this, but this is something that, as Senator Franken points out, we need to think about. If Internet gaming were legalized, would the NIGC have the capacity to regulate such gaming through Indian Country? And what would it take to ramp up personnel and technology to ensure that NIGC could regulate Tribal Internet gaming?

Ms. STEVENS. Well, without legislation, it is hard to say, but I will say that we are the only Federal agency who is solely dedicated to regulating Indian gaming. We have a well trained staff, experienced professionals who are well versed in Indian gaming. In the abstract, I couldn't say how much more money; it would depend on what roles or responsibilities are authorized in any piece of legislation or law that is passed by Congress. In the beginning of the agency it did take a while because it was a new agency, and we are not a new agency, so I imagine it wouldn't take as long as it did when the agency was first developed. But in the abstract I couldn't say; we would have to evaluate what the roles and responsibilities are in any law that is passed and evaluate our resources.

Senator UDALL. I appreciate very much those answers. As part of your report back to the Committee on compliance and how we are doing, if you could give me in your answer some kind of historical perspective: where we started out on compliance, how you have been doing; are the numbers going up, going down; are we having increasing problems. I think that would be really helpful to me, I know, and it might be helpful to other Committee members. Thank you for your testimony today and for your service. Thank you.

Ms. STEVENS. Thank you, Senator.

The CHAIRMAN. Thank you very much, Senator Udall, for your questions.

I want to thank Chairwoman Stevens very much for being here and for your responses to the Committee. We look forward to continuing to work with you. So thank you very much.

Ms. STEVENS. Thank you, Chairman Akaka, Vice Chairman Barrasso, and members of the Committee.

Now I would like to invite the second panel to the witness table.

Serving on our second panel is the Honorable Bruce ''Two Dogs'' Bozsum, Chairman of the Mohegan Tribe in Uncasville, Connecticut; Mr. Glen Gobin, Secretary of the Tulalip Tribes of Washington in Tulalip, Washington. Welcome to our panel and thank you very much for being here.

Chairman Bozsum, would you please proceed with your testimony?

STATEMENT OF HON. BRUCE "TWO DOGS" BOZSUM, CHAIRMAN, THE MOHEGAN TRIBE

Mr. BOZSUM. Thank you. Good afternoon, Chairman Akaka, Ranking Member Barrasso, and members of the Committee. My name is Bruce ''Two Dogs'' Bozsum. I am the Chairman of the Mohegan Tribe and also a ceremonial pipe carrier. It is a great honor to once again be here to present testimony to the Committee on the important subject of the regulation of Internet gambling.

Mr. Chairman, as you know, the Mohegan Tribe has been closely monitoring developments on the Internet gaming for the past several years. We have testified in both the Senate and the House, and engaged lawmakers developing Internet gaming policy. We also participated with our fellow Tribes in the National Indian Gaming Association and the National Congress of American Indians to develop a position for Indian Country.

Back home, our Tribe has a tradition of world-class regulation of our brick and mortar gaming facilities. We have invested a great deal of time to develop regulations for Internet gaming and these regulations now stand ready to be implemented and will meet or exceed the toughest regulations found anywhere in the world, including the new standards recently established in Nevada.

Internet gaming is a reality in today's digital world. Our Tribe is doing everything in our power to prepare for it. We also will never forget that our sovereignty is not negotiable. As a Tribal Chairman, I am informed by the ways of our people to first look to our past and traditions in order to see what lessons can be learned.

Applying this approach, it is clear that the current situation closely resembles the aftermath of the 1987 Cabazon Supreme Court decision. And just as the Cabazon case stopped Tribal opponents from claiming our gaming operations operated in a gray area, so has the December 23rd DOJ opinion now removed the uncertainty about whether the Wire Act prohibits Internet gaming, and it doesn't.

However, the DOJ opinion does not settle the details of the issue, just as the Cabazon case did not specifically address all of the details on how Indian gaming would actually operate. It fell upon Tribal leaders and Federal policymakers to decide how to move forward and fill in those details. Congress decided simply forging ahead after the Cabazon decision may have resulted in a patchwork of different systems. Key issues would have been unsettled for years and Tribes would have been left vulnerable to ongoing litigation.

Rather than settle for this haphazard patchwork of systems, some chose, instead, to establish a single coherent Federal policy for Tribal gaming in the Indian Gaming Regulatory Act, and while certainly not perfect and initially opposed by some Tribal leaders as an attack on sovereignty, IGRA has provided a framework for Tribal gaming which has become the biggest Tribal economic success story in our history.

I believe that in the wake of the game-changing DOJ opinion on Internet gaming, Tribal leaders and Federal legislators should work together to establish a single coherent Federal policy and I believe this to be a far superior approach to allowing a patchwork system with no guarantes that Tribal sovereignty and our hard-won gains would be protected. As a father of eight, I understand all too well the need for one set of rules.

Tribes should be extremely hesitant to entrust their economic futures to the 50 States, many of whom are in a financial crisis. Already everyone from commercial gaming interests to State lotteries are quickly maneuvering to establish Internet gaming systems in their State for their own advantage, and most of them are certain to give little, if any, consideration for the existing gaming compacts or the sovereign rights of the Tribes and their calculations, not to mention the thousands that depend on our Tribes for employment.

This chaotic approach is also not good for protecting consumers or preventing problems or underage gambling, either. We believe that the same high standard of consumer protections We have for our land-based gaming must be present for Internet gaming. While the intentions of those who advocate for a State-by-State approach to regulation are good, I simply believe the patchwork system without national standards would let too many minors, problem gamblers, and others fall through the cracks.

As I have said before, the Internet is national in its very nature. A Federal system developed with significant input from Tribes would be the most effective way to safeguard Tribal sovereignty and ensure that exclusive Tribal gaming rights are not violated. A Federal system would provide the best protection for consumers, the best safeguards against underage and problem gambling, and the strongest law enforcement protections against potential criminal activities. From a Tribal perspective, a good start would be to adhere to the principles unanimously adopted by NIGA regarding Internet gaming.

In conclusion, Mr. Chairman, starting with you, and members of the House and Senate have worked to explore many complex issues surrounding Internet gaming. Numerous hearings have been held, legislation has been proposed by you and others, and Tribal input has been sought. This good work has created a solid foundation and an environment where I believe a serious and well-informed effort to enact legislation this year can now take place. With a Federal system we will have friends such as yourself and the members of this Committee to fight to protect our rights.

We greatly appreciate your interest in this issue and look forward to working with you closely now and in the future.

[The prepared statement of Mr. Bozsum follows:]

PREPARED STATEMENT OF HON. BRUCE "TWO DOGS" BOZSUM, CHAIRMAN, THE
MOHEGAN TRIBE

Good afternoon Chairman Akaka, Vice Chairman Barrasso, and Members of the Committee. My name is Bruce "Two Dogs" Bozsum, and I am the Chairman of the Mohegan Tribe and also a Pipe Carrier. It is a great honor to once again be with you here today to present testimony on the important subject of Internet gaming and its regulation by the federal and tribal governments.

Mr. Chairman, as you know, the Mohegan Tribe has been closely monitoring developments on Internet gaming for the past several years. We have testified in both the Senate and the House, engaged lawmakers developing Internet gaming policy and participated with our fellow Tribes in the National Indian Gaming Association and the National Congress of American Indians to develop a position for Indian Country.

Back home, our Tribe has a tradition of requiring world-class regulation of our brick-and-mortar gaming facilities. We have invested a great deal of time to develop regulations for Internet gaming should they be necessary. These regulations now stand ready to be implemented, and will meet or exceed the toughest regulations found anywhere in the world, including the new standards recently established in Nevada.

Internet gaming is a reality in today's digital world. Our Tribe is doing everything in our power to prepare for it, and to look out for the best interests of Tribal governments and the commerce our Tribal nations depend upon. We will never forget that our sovereignty is not negotiable.

As a Tribal Chairman confronting the situations we face today, I am guided, by the ways of our Mohegan people, to first look to our past and traditions in order to see what lessons can be learned and applied to the present.

Applying this Mohegan approach to Internet gaming, it is clear that the current situation closely resembles the aftermath of the 1987 decision by the U.S. Supreme Court in the *Cabazon* case, which affirmed our rights as sovereign Tribal governments to authorize and regulate gaming. I believe we can learn much from studying this history and using it to guide our decisions today.

Just as the *Cabazon* case stopped tribal opponents from claiming our gaming operations operated in a "gray area" of the law, so has the December 23rd DOJ opinion now removed the "gray area" of uncertainty about whether the Wire Act prohibits Internet gaming. It doesn't.

However, the DOJ opinion does not settle all the details of the issue, just as the *Cabazon* case did not specifically address all of the details or significant questions of how Indian gaming would actually operate. As in the aftermath of *Cabazon*, it now falls upon Tribal leaders and federal policymakers to decide how to move forward and fill in those details.

After *Cabazon*, Congress in its wisdom believed that simply allowing the framework for Tribal gaming to evolve over time might result in a patchwork of different systems throughout the country. Key issues would have been unsettled for years, and Tribes would have been left vulnerable to ongoing litigation and the changing whims of political leadership.

Rather than settle for this haphazard patchwork of systems, federal legislators and some Tribal leaders chose instead to establish a single, coherent federal policy for Tribal gaming in the wake of the *Cabazon* decision. This policy is well-known to all of us now as the Indian Gaming Regulatory Act (IGRA). While certainly not perfect and initially opposed by several Tribal leaders as an attack on sovereignty, there is widespread agreement today that IGRA as enacted has provided a predictable and stable framework for Tribal gaming, which has become the biggest Tribal economic success story in our history.

I believe that in the wake of the game-changing DOJ opinion on Internet gaming, Tribal leaders and federal legislators should follow the same approach many did after *Cabazon*, and work together to establish a single, coherent federal policy to govern, with stability and predictability, what kinds of Internet gaming might be permitted and how Internet gaming should best be regulated. This would be far better than allowing a patchwork system to develop over the next two decades, state-by-state, lawsuit-by-lawsuit, and with no guarantees that Tribal sovereignty and our hard-won gains would be protected. Tribes should be extremely hesitant to entrust their economic futures to the tender mercies of the 50 states, many of whom are still in financial crises and looking for new sources of revenue. Already, everyone from commercial gaming interests to state lotteries is quickly maneuvering to establish Internet gaming systems in their state in order to make them work for their own advantage. Most of them are certain to give little, if any consideration for the existing gaming compacts or the sovereign rights of Tribes in their calculations. Not to mention the tens of thousands of American workers who depend on Tribes for employment.

This chaotic approach is not good for protecting consumers, or for preventing problem or underage gambling. I am proud that the Mohegan Tribe is a global leader in regulation to protect our customers and to prevent problem and underage gaming at our facilities. We believe that the same high standard of consumer protections we have for our land based gaming must control Internet gaming. While the intentions of those who advocate a state-by-state approach to regulation are good, I simply believe a patchwork system without national standards would let too many minors, problem gamblers, and others fall through the cracks.

The Internet is national in its very nature, and policy questions for gaming on the Internet are best addressed on a national level. A federal system, developed with consultation and significant input from Tribes, will be the most effective way to safeguard Tribal sovereignty and ensure that exclusive Tribal gaming rights are not violated by states and commercial gaming operators anxious to cash in on an Internet gaming boom. A federal system would provide the best protection for consumers, the best safeguards against underage and problem gambling, and the strongest law enforcement protections against potential criminal activities by those who choose to try to operate outside of the system that is lawfully established.

The creation of any federal system must be done in a fair and evenhanded way. From a Tribal perspective, a good start would be to adhere to the principles unanimously adopted by NIGA regarding Internet gaming. In addition, the Mohegan Tribe believes that any federal legislation must:

- Guarantee to Tribes the ability to accept, on Tribal lands, otherwise legal wagers from persons who are not themselves located on Tribal lands.
- Respect existing Tribal-state gaming compacts, including any rights of exclusivity.
- Recognize the difference between revenue sharing agreements and taxation, and ensure that Tribal sovereigns are not subject to taxation.
- Utilize existing Tribal government regulatory structures, which are working well and have an outstanding 25-plus year track record.
- Strictly enforce against unlicensed sites in order to protect players and the investment of Tribal and commercial gaming entities in legal, regulated sites.
- Be limited to poker-only.
- Facilitate the formation of Tribal Internet gaming coalitions across the country to better enable us to compete against large corporate commercial gaming concerns.

Mr. Chairman, you have been a leader among the many Members of the House and Senate who are working diligently to explore the many complex issues surrounding Internet gaming. Numerous hearings have been held, legislation has been proposed, and tribal input has been sought. This good work has created a solid foundation for understanding the key issues, and an environment where I believe a serious and well-informed effort to enact legislation this year in Washington can now take place. Given the new environment created by the DOJ opinion, I believe it is important that this federal action takes place soon. Tribes cannot risk the hazards of a patchwork system defined by the best interests of the states, lotteries, and commercial gaming. With a federal system, we will have friends such as yourself and the Members of this Committee to fight to protect our Tribal rights throughout the process.

We greatly appreciate your interest on this issue, and look forward to working with you closely now and in the future.

The CHAIRMAN. Thank you very much, Chairman, for your testimony.

I would like to call on the Secretary for your testimony. Would you please proceed, Mr. Gobin?

STATEMENT OF GLEN GOBIN, SECRETARY, TULALIP TRIBES OF WASHINGTON

Mr. GOBIN. Good afternoon, Chairman Akaka, Ranking Member Barrasso, and Committee members. My name is TE CHUHT, Glen Gobin, Secretary on the Tulalip Tribal Council. I would like to thank you for this opportunity to testify regarding regulation of gaming, from bricks and mortars to the Internet, and working to keep this issue at the forefront, recognizing the changes as a result of the DOJ opinion and the potential impacts in Indian Country.

I would like to say on a personal note, Chairman Akaka, I want to thank you for your leadership. I want to thank you for your leadership, in particular of this Committee, continuing to always bring issues like this that Tribes face in trying to bring resolution and understanding through the many years, and I thank you for your leadership.

On November 17, 2011, I testified before this Committee on Tulalip Tribe's position not supporting legalization of Internet gambling. That position was based on the potential negative impacts to existing Tribal gaming establishments and local economies, as well as the existing DOJ interpretation of the Wire Act prohibiting all forms of Internet gambling.

On December 23rd, 2011, the DOJ released a new interpretation of the Wire Act, reversing its long-held opinion, opening the door for States to move forward with Internet lottery sales within their respective States and with agreement between States and/or foreign nations. This new DOJ opinion clearly provides the opportunity for States to participate in Internet gambling activities within their States if they so choose. Some States have already begun to move forward and many more are actively working on setting up and establishing online systems.

Tribes have the ability to participate in the same activity, even though some may feel that Tribal participation is not yet fully defined. IGRA anticipated future gaming advancements and recognizes and allows for electronic, computer, and other technological aids, although the ability to fully access the Internet gaming market may be subject to interpretation.

Clarifying legislation will minimize conflict and litigation, which often puts Tribes and States at odds. It is for this reason that the six principles put forth by NIGA are critical for Indian Country. These principles represent core values that respect Tribal sovereignty.

Once more, we must emphasize that Tribes must be at the table to protect and promote these principles in any Federal legislation that might come forward. With Indian gaming representing over 40 percent of the gaming market, generating over $27.2 billion annually to this Nation's economy, not to mention the jobs and economic benefits Indian gaming brings to some of the most impoverished areas in the Country, it is inconceivable, given the recent DOJ opinion and with such sweeping changes in gaming being contemplated, that Tribes are not being consulted.

There is no pending legislation on Internet gambling at this time. However, past proposals created an Office of Internet Poker Oversight or designated the Secretary of Commerce with regulatory authority and oversight over Internet gaming. Tulalip feels, as do other Tribes in Indian Country, that there is only one Federal agency that has had any history of regulatory oversight of gaming, and that agency is the National Indian Gaming Commission.

The NIGC has over 20 years of extensive regulatory experience in gaming and it is the only Federal agency with that type of experience. The NIGC is an independent agency able to review, amend, and can promulgate regulations in an effective and timely manner. The NIGC has a long established history with Tribes and has continued to evolve and adapt to the changes within the gaming industry, transitioning from more traditional forms of gaming and mechanical slot machines to highly advanced server-based gaming systems, while ensuring compliance with all applicable Tribal, State, and Federal gaming standards.

The NIGC is well suited, more than any other Federal agency, to transition into Internet gaming. There is no other Federal agency that has any gaming or gaming-related experience, let alone Internet gaming experience. The NIGC understands and respects the government-to-government relationship with Tribal leadership and Tribal gaming regulators who have primary oversight of the day-to-day gaming activities. Creating a new agency will limit Tribes' opportunity and ability to compete, with their lack of understanding of Indian Tribes and Indian gaming. Creating any new agency or assigning Internet regulation to any existing agency would be burdensome and duplicative.

At this time, Tribes are still speculating and anticipating legislation that may be considered. However, since the new DOJ opinion, there is clearly a path defined for States to participate in Internet gaming, if they choose. Tribes must have equal footing to participate. By being inclusive of all affected stakeholders, we can preempt issues that are already foreseen in this arena and bring forward Internet gaming legislation to an open and collaborative process that protects the customer and the integrity of the games, ensuring that Tribes have equal opportunity to participate and compete, while protecting and respecting Tribal sovereignty.

Again, on behalf of the Tulalip Tribes, I thank the Committee for hearing some of the concerns from Tulalip Indian Country on the issues surrounding Internet gambling.

[The prepared statement of Mr. Gobin follows:]

PREPARED STATEMENT OF GLEN GOBIN, SECRETARY, TULALIP TRIBES OF WASHINGTON

Good afternoon Chairman Akaka, Ranking Member Barrasso and Committee Members, my name is, TE CHUHT, Glen Gobin, Secretary on the Tulalip Tribal Council. I would like to thank you for this opportunity to testify today regarding regulation of gaming, from bricks and mortar to the Internet, and working to keep this issue at the forefront, recognizing the changes as a result of the DOJ opinion and the potential impacts in Indian Country.

On November 17, 2011, I testified before this Committee on Tulalip Tribes position not supporting legalization of Internet Gambling. That position was based on the potential negative impacts to existing tribal gaming establishments and local economies, as well as the existing DOJ interpretation of the WIRE Act prohibiting of all forms of Internet gambling. On December 23, 2011, the DOJ released a new interpretation of the WIRE Act, reversing its long held opinion, opening the door for States to move forward with Internet lottery sales within their respective states, and with agreement between states and foreign nations. This new DOJ opinion clearly provides the opportunity for states to participate in Internet gambling activities within their states, if they choose. Some states have already begun to move forward and many more are actively working on setting up and establishing on-line systems.

Tribes have the ability to participate in this same activity; even though some may feel that tribal participation is not yet fully defined. IGRA anticipated future gaming advancements, and recognizes and allows for electronic, computer and other technological aids, although, the ability to fully access the Internet gaming market may be subject to interpretation. Clarifying legislation will minimize conflict and litigation, which often puts Tribes and states at odds. It is for this reason that the six principles put forth by NIGA are critical for Indian Country. These principles represent core values that respect tribal sovereignty by ensuring an Indian Tribes right to operate, regulate, tax, and license Internet gaming and these rights must not be subordinate to any non-federal authority; legislation must not open up IGRA for amendments; legislation must respect existing Tribal-State Compacts; legislation must ensure positive economic benefits to Indian Country; and legislation must ensure that Internet gambling authorized by Indian Tribes is available to customers in any locale where Internet gambling is not criminally prohibited.

Once more we emphasize that Tribes must be at the table to protect and promote these principles in any federal legislation that might come forward. With Indian gaming representing over 40 percent of the gaming market, generating over $27.2 billion annually to this nation's economy, not to mention the jobs and economic benefits Indian gaming brings to some of the most impoverished areas in the Country, it is inconceivable, given the recent change in the DOJ opinion, and with such sweeping changes in gaming being contemplated, that Tribes are not being consulted.

There is no pending legislation on Internet gambling at this time; however, past proposals created an Office of Internet Poker Oversight or designated the Secretary of Commerce with regulatory authority and oversight over Internet gaming. Tulalip feels, as do other tribes in Indian country, that there is only one federal agency that has any history of regulatory oversight of gaming, that agency is the National Indian Gaming Commission.

The NIGC has over 20 years of extensive regulatory experience in gaming, and it is the only federal agency with that experience. The NIGC is an independent agency, able to review, amend, and can promulgate regulations in an effective and timely manner. The NIGC has a long established history with Tribes, and has continued to evolve and adapt to the changes within the gaming industry, transitioning from more traditional forms of gaming and mechanical slot machines to highly advanced server based gaming systems while ensuring compliance with all applicable tribal, state, and federal gaming standards.

As an example, when IGRA became law in 1988, extensive controversy ensued as to whether the National Indian Gaming Commission would be effective in the regulation of Indian gaming. Many were concerned that organized crime and other corrupting influences would infiltrate Indian gaming. The NIGC, working in conjunction with Tribes, has proven to be fully capable of effective regulation of Indian gaming, dispelling these perceptions and fears.

The NIGC is well suited, more so than any other federal agency, to transition into Internet gaming. There is no other federal agency that has any gaming or gaming related experience, let alone Internet gaming experience. The NIGC understands and respects the government-to-government relationship with tribal leadership and tribal gaming regulators, who have primary oversight of day-to-day gaming activities. Creating a *new* agency will limit Tribes' opportunity and ability to compete, with their lack of understanding of Indian Tribes and Indian gaming. Creating any new agency or assigning Internet regulation to any existing agency would be burdensome and duplicative.

At this time, Tribes are still speculating and anticipating legislation that may be considered, however, since the new DOJ opinion, there is clearly a path defined for states to participate in Internet gaming if they choose. Tribes must have equal footing to participate. By being inclusive of all affected stakeholders we can preempt issues that are already foreseen in this arena, and bring forward Internet gaming legislation through an open and collaborative process that protects the customer and the integrity of the games; ensuring that Tribes have equal opportunity to participate and compete while protecting and respecting tribal sovereignty.

Again, on behalf of the Tulalip Tribes, I thank the committee for hearing some of the concerns from Tulalip and Indian Country on the issues surrounding Internet gambling.

The CHAIRMAN. Thank you very much, Mr. Secretary.

Chairman Bozsum, your Tribe, the Mohegan Tribe, has regulations that are more stringent than those established in Nevada. Do your regulations envision Tribes engaging in online gaming at the same level as other commercial gaming providers? Do you think that Tribes have the capacity to both participate in and regulate their online gaming operations?

Mr. BOZSUM. Thank you, Senator, Mr. Chairman. Great question. I believe we can. I know we can. I think we do a far better job than most commercial businesses out there. We take a lot of pride in our businesses and we make sure that the facility is safe, it is running, it is compliant. We have so much honor and pride with our own facilities that we want people to come there and feel safe, and you can't have that if you have a bad record or you don't think you can comply to the rules and regulations that gaming facilities should follow.

I think Tribes that are looking to get into the business of Internet gaming, there are good models out there right now that they could reach out to, as I have done, across the Country, meeting with other Tribes and other gaming facilities to get a feel of their regulations, their policies, and traveling overseas to meet with all of the biggest Internet companies that are out there to compare regulations and to talk about policies, and we have taken all that and pretty much have written a policy that we have that we are getting ready to actually share with you at some point soon. As soon as the rest of my board is available to go over it one more time with me, we will share that with you.

The CHAIRMAN. Thank you very much. We will look forward to that. Thank you.

Secretary Gobin, now that the Department of Justice opinion has impacted the Tribes' view on online gaming, what steps has Tulalip taken to be able to be ful participants in online gaming?

Mr. GOBIN. Thank you, Mr. Chairman. Since the last hearing that was held, Tulalip has been actively researching our access to the Internet, how we might partake in this and how it might be utilized not only in the gaming aspect, but how it might become a marketing tool or another way to bring customers in to a bricks and mortar facility.

Currently, within Washington State there is an RCW in place that prohibits Internet gambling in Washington State, so for us to implement the provision of the DOJ opinion, there would have to be an RCW change within Washington State. So we are not actively seeking any participation in that right now until that RCW changes.

The CHAIRMAN. Thank you very much.

Chairman Bozsum, should a Tribal Government's participation in online gaming be dependent on whether the State they reside in has opted in or opted out of participation in online gaming?

Mr. BOZSUM. Well, I will use myself as an example. I am the chief elected official for our Tribe in Connecticut, and if the governor decides to opt out, he has to meet with me, as one leader to another, as the head of the State there, and discuss what we can do on our reservation. It is my job as the elected official, and the rest of my board, to make those decisions on our reservation to uphold our sovereign rights.

The CHAIRMAN. Thank you very much for your response.

Vice Chairman Barrasso, do you have questions?

Senator BARRASSO. Thank you, Mr. Chairman. I just have one for both of the members of this panel.

Internet gaming is not an activity that can be confined within strict borders, and depending on what the future holds for Internet gaming, there may be instances where it might even cross Tribal boundaries, even if a Tribe doesn't participate in Internet gaming. I am curious if any of the Tribes represented on this panel have taken steps in anticipation of the possibility of regulating Internet gaming.

I think, Mr. Chairman, you had mentioned taking steps to prepare, and I am just interested in terms of what each of you are doing or have done in the possibility of regulating Internet gaming and what steps you have taken.

Mr. BOZSUM. Thank you. Like I mentioned, we have some great standards right now and some minimum control standards, and we have met with other Tribes and our goal is to form with the coalition, get Tribes together. Like the Senator mentioned earlier, Senator Franken, about the Tribes that don't have an opportunity right now, because of their location, to participate in any gaming, I look at it as an opportunity to bring those Tribes in. It is the Internet; you don't have to build a facility.

If we create with our coalition a hub, at some point we offer that to other Tribes to tap into to create the revenues and the income for them through us, with our regulations that we have in place right now, and I look at it as an opportunity for everybody in Indian Country to have that opportunity. It gives them the freedom to support their health, their education benefits, stand alone and take care of those issues on their own, and free up some money back in Federal grants, back to other needy issues or other needy Tribes, whoever may need that money. It is better to stand up on your own feet and take care of your own.

Senator BARRASSO. Mr. Secretary?

Mr. GOBIN. Thank you. I think back 24 years, and Tribes started 24 years with the requirement for gaming to be in place and you had Indian gaming, IGRA in place, and it set up a regulatory process. Tribes have developed a very highly effective and highly technical regulatory process through our Tribal gaming agencies, in conjunction with the State and in conjunction with the NIGC over the last 24 years to protect and ensure and safeguard the games that are in place. There was a system established; there were games that were developed; there were games that were put in place, and every time there was a change, there was a new procedure put in place, a new control that was put in place, and it always had constant oversight from those three agencies.

I see no difference, as we move forward into the future, for Internet gaming. We are going to evolve as we always have done, and we are going to move forward in a positive manner and protect those games, because those revenues drive our government services and fund our governmental operations. It is hard to imagine not having those systems in place as we move into Internet gaming. But yet that process is not defined. We are not sure as to how that is, so my Tribe is not prepared yet with any regulations because we are unsure of what the parameters are going to be, how we are going to access that market for sure. So to say that we are prepared with full regulatory aspect, we are not, but I have full confidence that we have the capability to do it.

Senator BARRASSO. Thank you.

Thank you, Mr. Chairman.

The CHAIRMAN. Thank you very much, Senator Barrasso.

Senator Franken?

Senator FRANKEN. Thank you. I am sorry I had to step out for your testimony, but I have a few questions. This is for both witnesses.

As I said in my opening statement, I have seen firsthand the positive impacts of Indian gaming, both in my home State and across the Country. Can you each talk about the state of your communities before and after your Tribes started gaming operations?

Mr. BOZSUM. Thank you, Senator. Our Tribe back in Uncasville, Connecticut, we were pretty spread out. Everything was taken from us; we were down to half an acre of land with a church on it, so we were spread out throughout the community. And when the State, when things moved forward and we had the opportunity to start gaming in Connecticut, we were able to stop receiving any Federal grants or funds to support our Tribal members, so we took our funding from the casino or any extra money we had and supported our Tribal members with health and education benefits.

Those were two of the most important things that we look at in our Tribe. The casino may not be there forever, but a great education can go a long way, and the health of our Tribal members and our elders, that is where we like to invest the bulk of our finances. I look at doctors, lawyers; we have everything covered that you can imagine out there with all of our children and some of our adults who went back to school. So our reinvestment is back into our Tribal members.

And then the community that we live in, with our fire department that we have, we help, we respond to all the community needs that they have; we support a lot of charities.

Senator FRANKEN. I am sorry to interrupt. I really wanted a sort of, and, Mr. Gobin, you can talk to this, or you can continue, just the contrast from before and after.

Mr. BOZSUM. We are very healthy. I mean healthy like I am living proof of what Indian gaming can do. I was diagnosed with something long ago and the Tribe stepped up and took care of me, so here is living proof of what Indian gaming can do right here. I should have been dead. I am not.

Senator FRANKEN. You look great.

Mr. BOZSUM. Thank you.

[Laughter.]

Mr. BOZSUM. So do you.

[Laughter.]

Senator FRANKEN. Thank you.

Mr. Gobin, you look great too.

Mr. GOBIN. Thank you.

[Laughter.]

Mr. GOBIN. Thank you for the question, as well.

[Laughter.]

Mr. GOBIN. I think back in my lifetime. I was born in 1956. And the changes from my reservation, my memories go back to growing up in the 1960s, there were no jobs, there were no economic activities. Our Tribal Government had a small leasing program where we took the prime property around Tulalip Bay, waterfront property, and we leased it to non-Indians to come out, and it drove our revenue stream that funded our government. Very small, very minimal, but it provided a governmental revenue stream that came in.

As things evolved, our leadership continued to struggle and tried to find ways to generate more money, but the day-to-day lives of the people were making a living off of fishing or working in the woods, logging or cutting shake boards, if that was the case. I remember many meals. We ate deer meat until summertime came, and then we ate fish, and that was our cycle. And as gaming came on, it created a revenue stream for the Tribes to now start to control their own destiny. As the revenues came in, it was reinvested back in funding governmental programs that were short-funded or developing new governmental programs, providing services to the people.

I graduated high school in 1975, not with the best GPA, so I was not the highest qualified to go to college, but my Tribe had no means to do that. Today, all four of my kids have gone to college, the last one will graduate this year, and the Tribe has paid for that with these gaming revenues through this whole process. They provide for elders, they provide homes, they build infrastructure, we help fund I–5 interchange projects, we help fund roads, we do business development all with the revenues that come from gaming; they go back into the community, they go back into the surrounding communities, and the prosperity on the reservation has changed. But not for all. There are still issues that are out there. As every government will know, there is not always enough money to go around to meet all the needs of the people.

Senator FRANKEN. Thank you, gentlemen.

The CHAIRMAN. Thank you, Senator Franken. Senator Udall?

Senator UDALL. Thank you, Chairman Akaka.

I know this hearing isn't about the draft legislation that was put out there. The Chairman has put out a draft piece of legislation on online gaming. I believe it has been given to the NIGC; it is on the website of this Committee. I believe it is out front and available. Any thoughts that you all have on it?

Mr. BOZSUM. I haven't had a chance to review it with my staff yet, but I am looking forward to it and I would love to comment on it as soon as we get that opportunity back home.

Senator UDALL. And we would love to hear your comments.

Secretary Gobin?

Mr. GOBIN. Unfortunately, I didn't fly in until late last night, and I have not had a chance to see it or review it. I did pick up a copy here this afternoon, so I will be looking forward to going through and providing comment as well.

Senator UDALL. Okay. In case you had anything to say, I just wanted to give you an opportunity.

You know, we have had a little bit of a discussion on the positive effects of gaming, and I would say that almost all of the Tribes in New Mexico that game feel that it has been very positive for their Tribes, and I am reminded of an old time Pueblo leader that had seen his Tribe for over 80 years, and he related to me some of the things that he thought were very positive.

He said in all the years up until gaming came, he had 50 percent unemployment at the Pueblo, and he said today, after we have opened our gaming establishment, we are down to zero. And not only have we provided jobs for every able-bodied person, we are able to give employment to non-Indians. So he felt very good about that. There is always, he said, talk about lack of educational opportunities, just as the Chairman said. Now this Pueblo, he said, is able to give college scholarships to every young person that wants to go to college, that can get in. Same with health care facilities, putting health care facilities as a result of the income; paving roads.

So I think there have been some very positive developments as a result of Tribes engaging in gaming, and I don't blame the Tribes for wanting to look at each development that comes along and see how that is going to impact their investment in gaming. So that is important to meet to hear from Tribes as to what their reaction is to this draft legislation and any other things that they see that is out there.

So, with that, Chairman Akaka, I know we have a vote on, and I am happy to help out in terms of keeping the hearing going, or however you want to do it. Thank you. I am going to yield back at this point.

The CHAIRMAN. Thank you very much, Senator Udall.

I want to thank this panel very much for your responses and your testimony as well.

I am going to ask for a recess at this moment, and whoever comes back first will take the third panel at that time.

But, again, I want to say thank you for sharing with us what you have been doing with your Tribes. It is very, very helpful and it is good to know that these gaming programs are really helping the Tribes as well. So I thank you very much for being here and at this time call for a brief recess. Thank you.

[Recess.]

The CHAIRMAN. I want to welcome our third panel here.

We have Mr. Jamie Hummingbird, who is the Chairperson of the National Tribal Gaming Commissioners and Regulators in Tahlequah, Oklahoma; also, Ms. Elizabeth Homer, attorney at Homer Law in Washington, D.C.; the Honorable Jon Potter, former Congressman and President of Porter Gordon Silver Communications in Las Vegas, Nevada; and Mr. Eugene Johnson, Senior Vice President for Marketing and Online Studies for the Spectrum Gaming Group in Linwood, New Jersey.

I want to welcome all of you here today.

Mr. Hummingbird, Chairman Hummingbird, would you please proceed with your statement and your testimony?

STATEMENT OF JAMIE HUMMINGBIRD, CHAIRMAN, NATIONAL TRIBAL GAMING COMMISSIONERS/REGULATORS ASSOCIATION

Mr. HUMMINGBIRD. Thank you, Chairman Akaka, members of the Committee. My name is Jamie Hummingbird and I am the Director of the Gaming Commission for Cherokee Nation. I also serve as the Chairman of the National Tribal Gaming Commissioners and Regulators Association. Please accept my most sincere appreciation on behalf of the National Tribal Gaming Commissioners and Regulators for allowing testimony before the Committee regarding the state of gaming regulation in Indian Country today and how it may change in the future.

The National Tribal Gaming Commissioners and Regulators is an organization devoted to the education and advancement of gaming regulation within Tribal gaming facilities. Comprised of Tribal gaming regulators across the Country, the organization serves as a center for training of regulatory professionals and the free exchange of regulatory best practices.

Nearly a quarter century ago, Congress passed the Indian Gaming Regulatory Act, and Tribes and Tribal gaming regulators have progressed along with the gaming industry, often setting the pace in regulation development.

IGRA incorporated many of the principles of regulation that Tribes followed at the time, which continue to shape the face of gaming regulation in Indian Country today. This success was made possible by following the core values at the heart of every Tribal gaming regulatory authority: protecting Tribal assets, ensuring the integrity of the gaming requirement, and requiring accountability of the gaming operations. As gaming technology has evolved in brick and mortar, these values held firm and will continue to guide us as we look to the next phase of evolution in Internet gaming.

Today there are approximately 85 countries that have legalized some form of Internet gaming, whether in the form of Internet cafes as part of a brick and mortar facility, or through a mobile device, which represents an estimated $30 billion industry. Jurisdictions such as Alderney and British Columbia have chosen to establish iGaming laws and favor strict regulatory controls that govern Internet gaming activities.

Internet gaming has drawn proponents and opponents from State and Tribal Governments, as well as various Federal departments and members of Congress. While some States have taken steps toward authorizing Internet gaming, there is an increasing louder call for a Federal solution.

In the years since 2006 and the passage of the Unlawful Internet Gaming Enforcement Act, the American Internet gaming landscape at the Federal level has undergone a paradigm shift from being considered criminal-prohibitory, to being civil-regulatory in nature. Members of the Congress who initially opposed iGaming now support Internet gaming under certain conditions.

Any legislation considered at the Federal level must provide parity to Tribes by providing Tribes and States equal treatment under any law that is enacted.

Tribal gaming regulatory authorities, or TGRAs, jealously protect the integrity of any and all gams offered by the Tribal gaming facilities. This would be no less true should Internet gaming become a viable option for Tribes.

Many existing regulations already employed by TGRAs will lend themselves to be used in the digital realm. TGRAs can learn from jurisdictions where Internet gaming is in operation to develop a set of requirements that will fit their unique environment. Game protection and the security of personal and financial information is paramount for TGRAs, and the ability of games to be certified legal and secure is essential.

The regulations governing the activity of brick and mortar facilities can be adapted to fit Internet gaming operations, particularly the regulations that ensure the financial accountability of the gaming operation and demonstrate the ability of gaming operations to meet all financial obligations.

Under legislation enacted, whether at the State or Federal level, TGRAs will be asked to ensure that only those persons within their authorized jurisdiction may participate in Tribal gaming sites. TGRAs will require the verification of a player's location through the process of geo-location to determine whether or not that person is able to legally participate in the Tribe's Internet gaming site. Geo-location will also play an instrumental role in verifying the location of authorized players using mobile devices.

The societal issues of underage gambling and problem gambling are matters that TGRAs will be required to address, much as they do in Tribal brick and mortar facilities. These concerns are best addressed by the regulations TGRAs will require in establishing Internet gaming accounts and the process by which gaming activity will be monitored to identify any potential patterns indicative of problem gambling.

Tribal investments in technology, infrastructure, and operating capital must be made. Additionally, investment in human capital will also be necessary. The need for qualified and experienced staff is of vital importance to the success of any Internet gaming venture.

The success of any business venture lies in preparation, and in the case of Internet gaming, preparation includes formulating the proper regulatory model to complement the legislative side of the equation. Tribes have been responding to a changing gaming market since the enactment of IGRA, and our Tribal Governments and regulators often set the standard for new gaming technologies and regulations. We are prepared to do so again should Internet gaming become legalized.

Indian gaming success is due in part to the presence of strong regulatory bodies. Through the years of practical application, Tribes have garnered the necessary expertise and experience to overcome the challenges that will be presented with the passage of Internet gaming legislation. The success we have collectively achieved since the passage of IGRA clearly shows that Tribes are more than capable of being strong participants and regulators in the Internet gaming industry.

On behalf of the national Tribal Gaming Commissioners and Regulators, I thank you for the opportunity to present this testimony and am open to any questions you may have.

[The prepared statement of Mr. Hummingbird follows:]

PREPARED STATEMENT OF JAMIE HUMMINGBIRD, CHAIRMAN, NATIONAL TRIBAL
GAMING COMMISSIONERS/REGULATORS ASSOCIATION

Chairman Akaka, Vice-Chairman Barrasso, members of the Committee, my name is Jamie Hummingbird. I am the Director of the Cherokee Nation Gaming Commission. I also serve as Chairman of the National Tribal Gaming Commissioners/Regulators Association. It is in this capacity in which I address you today.

Please accept my most sincere appreciation on behalf of the National Tribal Gaming Commissioners/Regulators Association for allowing testimony before the Committee regarding the state of gaming regulation in Indian Country today and how it may change in the future.

The National Tribal Gaming Commissioners/Regulators is an organization devoted to the education and advancement of gaming regulation within tribal gaming facilities. Comprised of tribal gaming regulators across the country, the organization serves as a center for the training of regulatory professionals and the free exchange of regulatory best practices. As the gaming industry has evolved, incorporating the latest in technology for game play as well as the associated systems that complete the gaming experience, so too have tribal gaming regulators grown in their capacity to successfully regulate tribal gaming.

Brief History of Indian Gaming Regulation

In the late 1970s and early 1980s, Indian tribes across the country began operating bingo facilities as a means of providing funds for tribal assistance programs. The success of these facilities quickly drew the attention and ire of local and state government officials who sought to enforce state laws on Indian land.

Tribes, believing their decision to operate gaming facilities was an exercise in tribal sovereignty, resisted state incursions of tribal gaming facilities. The debate regarding the legality of tribes offering gaming on tribal lands culminated in the 1987 Supreme Court decision in *California v. Cabazon Band of Mission Indians* wherein the Court held that tribes could operate and regulate gaming on tribal lands.

As a result of this landmark decision, the Congress passed the Indian Gaming Regulatory Act (IGRA) in an attempt to balance state and tribal gaming interests. In its drafting of IGRA, the Select Committee on Indian Affairs set out to "preserve the right of tribes to self-government" by recognizing tribes' sovereign rights to determine the course of their own affairs, including the means by which they would regulate their respective gaming operations.

IGRA required tribes to adopt gaming ordinances to provide the regulatory structure that would govern tribal gaming facilities. In order to achieve this task, tribes and tribal gaming regulatory authorities (TGRA) assessed their particular gaming environment and formulated regulations that provided for the licensing of gaming facilities, employees and vendors, approval of games, surveillance, security, and auditing of gaming operation financials. In addition, tribes and TGRAs were called upon to ensure the protection of the environmental, public health and safety of the gaming facility employees and patrons.

The IGRA incorporated many of the principles of regulation that tribes followed at the time, which continue to shape the face of gaming regulation in Indian Country today. Every TGRA, at its heart, contains the core values of protecting tribal assets, ensuring the integrity of the gaming environment, and requiring accountability of the gaming operations.

Over the years, the success of tribal gaming prompted more tribes to engage in gaming. Realizing the need for consistency and in an effort to assist those tribes that were new to the industry, a task force of tribal regulators within the National Indian Gaming Association and the National Congress of American Indians developed a model set of internal controls that provided base operating standards by which any gaming operation could be effectively regulated. The choice to adopt these standards and the language that would be contained in a tribal set of internal controls was left to each tribe to determine. However, In 1999, these standards were adapted by the National Indian Gaming Commission (NIGC) to become the Minimum Internal Control Standards (MICS) that all tribes were required to abide by.

In addition to the MICS, TGRAs utilize several other methods to ensure compliance of tribal gaming facilities, few of which match the importance of the employment of qualified personnel. Tribes invest heavily in the training of regulatory staff and highly value those with experience in law enforcement, accounting, and information technology.

By remaining at the forefront of innovation in gaming and gaming regulation, tribal gaming operations have become as sophisticated as any non-Indian gaming jurisdiction, if not more so. It is in this tradition of innovation and regulation that tribes will enter the digital realm of Internet gaming.

History of Internet Gaming

Although the subject of iGaming, also called online gaming or Internet gaming, has seen increased debate in numerous circles over the last few years, the industry has its origins in the mid-1990s when the government of Antigua and Barbuda passed laws allowing online casinos to offer the first gambling games on the Internet. Shortly thereafter, the Kahanawake Gaming Commission in Canada was established, controling and regulating online gaming activity from the Mohawk Territory of Kahnawake.

Today, there are approximately eighty-five (85) countries that have legalized some form of iGaming, whether in the form of Internet cafes, as part of a brick-and-mortar facility, or through a mobile device (e.g. smartphone/tablet), representing an estimated $30 billion industry. Jurisdictions such as Malta, the Isle of Man, the U.K., Italy, Germany, Alderney, and British Columbia have chosen to establish iGaming laws and favor strict regulatory controls to govern iGaming activities.

Seeing the "new" communication medium called the Internet was going to be used not only for commerce but also for gambling, some states enacted anti-gaming laws prohibiting iGaming in the late 1990's and early 2000's. One state—Nevada—staying true to its gaming roots, enacted legislation legalizing Internet gaming in 2001 and empowered the Nevada Gaming Control Board to enact regulations to pave the way for iGaming commerce to begin.

In 2003, Antigua lodged a complaint with the World Trade Organization (WTO) stating that, although American policy did not prohibit iGaming, the American government refused to allow foreign casinos to accept wagers from U.S. players. In a first-of-its-kind ruling, the WTO stated that the United States laws prohibiting iGaming violated international trade laws. The Bush Administration condemned the ruling over a concern that American social policy would be dictated by foreign powers.

Despite this activity, nothing happened on the U.S. iGaming scene until 2006 when the Unlawful Internet Gaming Enforcement Act (UIGEA) was passed, being attached to a must-pass port security act literally at the midnight hour. Although the name suggests the act of iGaming was made illegal by this piece of federal legislation, in actuality the practice of allowing financial transactions at iGaming sites by financial institutions was the center of the legislation; the legislation also did not pertain to intra-state transactions.

On April 15, 2011, the U.S. Department of Justice (DOJ) seized the Internet domain names of five of the largest online gaming operators, a day that has become know as "Black Friday". A month later, on May 23rd, a Maryland grand jury ordered the seizure of approximately a dozen more Internet domain names of other companies offering iGaming, a day that has been labeled "Blue Monday." These actions marked the first significant action taken against iGaming since the passage of the UIGEA.

In spite of the activity earlier in the year, iGaming interests continued to pursue avenues to legalize iGaming. A major obstacle in the way of the legalization of iGaming was the applicability of the 1961 Wire Act. It was long thought that the Wire Act prohibited the transmission of wagers across state lines. However, the DOJ changed this mindset with the issuance of a legal opinion on 23 December 2011 wherein the agency reversed its long-held position stating the Wire Act only applied to sports wagering and did not cover iGaming, particularly on-line poker, casino games and lotteries.

Throughout this time, iGaming has drawn proponents and opponents from state and tribal governments as well as various federal departments and members of Congress. Some states, besides Nevada, have taken firm steps towards authorizing iGaming (some with the active participation of tribal governments) and there is an increasingly louder call from all areas of the gaming industry for a federal solution to be enacted.

Federal and State Legislation

In the years since 2006 and the UIGEA, the American iGaming landscape at the federal level has undergone a paradigm shift from iGaming being considered criminal-prohibitory to being civil-regulatory in nature. Members of Congress who initially opposed iGaming now support allowing iGaming under certain conditions.

At the same time, commercial casinos in New Jersey and Nevada, as well as advocacy groups such as the American Gaming Association, have switched to supporting iGaming—again, under certain conditions.

Various bills have been introduced in the House of Representatives and in the Senate that would essentially undo the effects of the UIGEA. Some bills contained provisions that provided a basis for tribes to build on while others contained language that either put tribes at a disadvantage to commercial casinos or were outright contrary to tribes and tribal sovereignty. In 2010, Representatives Barney Frank, John Campbell, and Senator Robert Menendez each offered bills to regulate iGaming, which finally provided tribes with a place at the table.

Any legislation considered at the federal level must provide parity to tribes by providing tribes and states equal treatment under any law that is enacted.

The majority of states are forecasting budget shortfalls in the coming years and are looking for ways to add to state coffers. This has led to a trend amongst states to consider authorizing iGaming as a means to that end.

The following are examples of some of the steps taken by the various states:

- Nevada—The State legislature authorized iGaming in 2001; enacted iGaming regulations in 2011; began accepting applications for online operator gaming licenses in February 2012 and have begun issuing licenses to iGaming operators.
- New Jersey—The State legislature authorized iGaming in 2010, but the bill was vetoed by Governor Christie; a new bill has unanimously passed the state senate Budget and Appropriations Committee with a vote expected in the Fall of 2012.
- Iowa—A study was conducted and a report issued on the possible regulation of iGaming in Iowa, with the recommendation for approval; the Iowa Senate passed a bill on 13 March 2012 authorizing iGaming; the Iowa House voted against the bill three days later on 16 March 2012.
- California—The current form of California's iGaming bill (S. 1463), which would authorize Internet poker, was referred to committee at the end of March and is currently pending.
- Delaware—In June, the Governor has signed House Bill 333 into law allowing for all forms of gaming—poker, blackjack, slot machines, and lottery tickets—to be offered online to Delaware citizens.

Tribes across the country have debated whether the introduction of iGaming into tribal jurisdictions will be a detriment to current brick-and-mortar facilities or if it is a new segment of the market that, if left untouched, could be a competitive disadvantage and/or result in lost revenue to the tribe.

At the heart of the controversy—besides the overall issues surrounding tribal sovereignty—is the concern regarding the potential impact any legislation may have on tribal exclusivity as contained in tribal-state compacts. Despite this concern—or perhaps because of it—many tribes are carefully assessing their options in the instance iGaming is authorized, whether at the state or federal level.

State operated lotteries are another side of the iGaming issue. Several state lotteries have looked to the Internet to boost sales and have begun offering scratch-off tickets and other lottery tickets online. Seven (7) other states and the District of Columbia are also pursuing Internet lottery games.

Regulation of iGaming

As stated earlier, TGRAs jealously protect the integrity of any and all games offered by the tribal gaming facilities. This would be no less true should iGaming become a viable option for tribes.

In order to ensure the integrity of iGaming, TGRAs will be called upon to introduce new regulations over aspects of iGaming beyond those relating to game play.

Under any legislation that is enacted, whether at the state or federal level, TGRAs will be tasked with ensuring that only those persons within their authorized jurisdiction are able to conduct gaming transactions in tribal iGaming sites. Depending on the legal parameters defined in the legislation, this may be accomplished in one or two ways: residency verification and/or geo-location. Should the legislation prescribe a limited coverage area, say a reservation, state borders, or countries in which iGaming is not permitted, TGRAs will require a prospective player to attest to his/her residence and then, through the process of geo-location, the process of verifying a person's physical location, determine whether or not that person is able to legally access the tribe's iGaming site. Geo-location will also play an instrumental role in verifying the location of authorized players utilizing mobile devices such as smartphone or tablet computers.

The societal issues of underage gambling and problem gambling are issues that TGRAs will be required to address. These concerns are best addressed by the regulations TGRAs will require to establish iGaming accounts and the process by which gaming activity will be monitored to identify any potential patterns indicative of problem gambling. TGRAs may require additional information and/or documentation from prospective players to verify not only their identity but their ability to legally engage in iGaming.

Many other tools that will be needed by TGRAs to effectively regulate iGaming currently exist. TGRAs have methods to thoroughly investigate gaming and gaming related vendors. However, these methods may require slight modifications depending on the path taken by the tribal gaming operations, particularly if partnerships with overseas vendors are pursued.

The technical standards and game testing requirements employed by TGRAs will also lend themselves to being used in the digital arena. Far from having to reinvent the wheel, TGRAs can learn from jurisdictions where iGaming is in operation to develop a set of requirements that will fit their unique environment. Game protection is paramount to TGRAs and the ability of games to be certified as legal and secure is essential.

These standards will also provide the first line of defense in protecting information obtained from prospective players. The confidentiality of personal and financial information provided by prospective players as they establish iGaming accounts cannot be compromised.

The rules and regulations and internal controls used to govern the activity of the brick-and-mortar facilities can be adapted to fit iGaming operations. The regulations that ensure the financial accountability of the gaming operation and demonstrate the ability of the iGaming operation to meet all financial obligations.

Each of these aspects will require an investment on behalf of any tribe electing to offer iGaming. Investments in technology, infrastructure, and operating capital must be made. Yet that is not the extent to which tribes will need to invest; investment in human capital will also be necessary. The need for qualified and experienced staff is of vital importance to the success of an iGaming venture.

Conclusion

The success of any business venture lies in preparation. In the case of iGaming, preparation includes formulating the proper regulatory model to complement the legislative side of the equation. Tribes have been responding to a changing gaming market since the enactment of IGRA. Our tribal governments and regulators often set the standard for new gaming technologies and regulations. We are prepared to do so again should iGaming expansion occur.

The success of Indian gaming operations is due, in part, to the presence of strong regulatory bodies. Through years of practical application, tribes have garnered the necessary expertise and experience to overcome the challenges that will be presented with the passage of iGaming legislation. The success we have collectively achieved since the passage of IGRA clearly shows that tribes are more than capable of being strong participants and regulators in the gaming industry.

On behalf of the National Tribal Gaming Commissioners and Regulators, I thank you for the opportunity to present this testimony, and am open to any questions you may have.

The CHAIRMAN. Thank you very much, Chairman Hummingbird, for your testimony.

Ms. Homer, will you please proceed with your testimony?

STATEMENT OF ELIZABETH LOHAH HOMER, ATTORNEY, HOMER LAW

Ms. HOMER. Thank you for inviting me to testify today about these issues. My name is Elizabeth Lohah Homer. I am a member of the Osage Nation of Oklahoma and a practicing attorney who once served as a special attorney at the Criminal Division of the Department of Justice, the Office of American Indian Trust at the Interior Department, and, finally, as the Vice Chair of the National Indian Gaming Commission.

For nearly a decade now, I have served Tribal clients in the gaming law arena, with a particular focus on gaming regulatory matters. My clients include Tribal councils, Tribal regulatory agencies, Tribal gaming enterprises, and Tribal organizations such as the National Indian Gaming Association.

Although I draw heavily on this experience in my testimony today, the views I express today are my own and are not attributable to anybody else.

In much of Indian Country, though not all, the advent of gaming has meant the difference between a future of seemingly hopeless poverty, depression, and despair, and a future of growth, hope, and opportunity. Tribal gaming revenues have translated into increased Tribal Governmental capacity, new and expanded Tribal Governmental services, and an enhanced quality of life in many parts of Indian Country.

This Committee deserves credit for making this change possible, but I would add that where the success truly lies is in the responsible manner in which Tribal Governments have undertaken their gaming activities and the wise choices and investments that they have made.

Today we stand at a crossroads. The technological revolution, the advent of the Internet and broad public access to the information highway compel us to consider the future of Tribal gaming. As the Committee deliberates the ramifications of Internet gaming and considers legislation related to it, please bear in mind that while the means may be new, may be novel, the Internet, the legal, regulatory, and policy issues underlying Internet gaming are quite familiar. We have been dealing with those same issues for a very long time now.

In IGRA, Congress established a unique system of shared regulatory responsibilities among the Federal Government, the States, and Tribal Governments. To carry out the Tribal interests, Tribal Governments have established Tribal gaming regulatory agencies. To carry out the Federal interest, Congress created the National Indian Gaming Commission. Together the NIGC and Tribal gaming regulatory agencies provide a two-tiered framework for the regulation of Tribal gaming in a structure that is consistent with core principles of Federal Indian policy.

Any bifurcation of the Federal regulatory oversight responsibilities between the NIGC and another Federal agencies would be imprudent. Under current law, the respective roles of the NIGC and Tribal Governments are clearly established and defined. Communication systems are in place, administrative processes and enforcement mechanisms are established, and basically this is a system that works.

Assigning the administration of a statute or statutory provisions peculiar to Tribal gaming to multiple Federal agencies will inevitably create a host of problems and uncertainties. It would also increase the potential for interagency conflict and subject Tribal Governments to oversight by Federal agency personnel inexperienced not only in relation to Indian affairs, Indian law and policy and the Federal-Indian relationship, but in the regulation of gaming.

The NIGC has nearly two decades of gaming regulatory experience, and its members and staff understand the unique constitutional status of Indian Tribes as sovereigns, as well as the special political relationship between Tribal Governments and the United States. No other Federal agency possesses comparable experience or expertise in the context of Tribal gaming. Unquestionably, the NIGC is the ideal Federal agency candidate to administer any Tribal Internet gaming legislation. It is the only Federal agency that possesses the regulatory infrastructure to quickly and efficiently assume a gaming regulatory oversight role in relation to Tribal Internet gaming.

Practically speaking, it takes years, sometimes decades, to establish a functioning Federal agency. A new agency must assemble a competent staff, promulgate rules and regulations, meet all regulatory requirements applicable to every Federal agency, and commence operation. For example, it took nearly five years following the enactment of IGRA for the NIGC to actually commence operations. A similar delay in staffing a new agency and gearing up that agency to begin regulating Tribal Internet gaming could prove economically disastrous for Tribal Governments that are intended to benefit by such law. The NIGC would not be hindered by a long start-up time or the kinds of delays involved in the formation of new agencies.

Finally, and I see that my time is up, if I might just add, a key difference between the NIGC and other Federal agencies is the NIGC status as an independent regulatory agency of the United States. This cloaks the NIGC with the necessary independence and flexibility to carry out its Federal oversight functions in a stable and consistent manner, not subject to abrupt shifts in leadership, policy, resources, and organization.

Thank you very much. Thank you for your patience.

[The prepared statement of Ms. Homer follows:]

PREPARED STATEMENT OF ELIZABETH LOHAH HOMER, ATTORNEY, HOMER LAW

Chairman Akaka, Vice-Chairman Barrasso, and Members of the Committee:

Thank you for inviting me to testify this afternoon with regard to regulatory issues that arise in the context of tribal Internet gaming. My name is Elizabeth Lohah Homer. I am a member of the Osage Nation and a practicing attorney. I founded Homer Law shortly after leaving federal service, where I served as a special attorney with the Criminal Division at the U.S. Department of Justice, Director of the Office of American Indian Trust with the U.S. Department of the Interior, and finally, a three-year term appointment to the National Indian Gaming Commission (NIGC), where I served as the Vice-chair from July 1999 to July 2002.

During my tenure with the NIGC, the Commission undertook several important regulatory initiatives, including the revision of regulatory definitions for gaming activities; revision of the minimum internal control standards; and the development of an interpretive rule concerning environment, public health, and safety standards for tribal gaming operations. We also oversaw the expansion of the NIGC to include a field office structure and an increase in the agency's staffing level.

For nearly a decade now, I have primarily served tribal clients in the gaming law arena, with a particular focus on regulatory matters. My clients include tribal councils, tribal regulatory agencies, tribal gaming enterprises, and tribal organizations such as the National Indian Gaming Association. Although I draw heavily on this experience in my testimony today, the views I express this afternoon are mine alone and should not be attributed in any way to anyone other than me.

In much of Indian Country, though not all, the advent of gaming has meant the difference between a future of seemingly hopeless poverty, depression, and despair and one of growth, advancement, and promise. Tribal gaming revenues have provided tribal governments the means to make investments that could hardly be imagined when I graduated from college and began my first job with the Osage Nation in 1979. These revenues translate directly into increased tribal governmental capacity and new and expanded tribal governmental programs and services that range from law enforcement to fire and emergency services to health care, education, roads, clean water, sanitation facilities, and the list goes on and on and on. This Committee deserves a lot of credit for what has and continues to happen throughout Indian Country, but it is the responsible manner in which the tribal leadership has undertaken gaming and the wise investments that have been made with the revenue that has made tribal gaming successful and beneficial.

Today, we stand at a crossroads similar in many ways to the one confronted in the mid-1980s just prior to the enactment of the Indian Gaming Regulatory Act

(IGRA) in 1988, where important decisions must be made and time is of the essence. The technological revolution, the advent of the Internet and broad public access to the information highway—these things are changing the world. It is an exciting time, but it is a challenging one as well. As the Committee deliberates the ramifications of Internet gaming and considers legislation related to it, I urge you to take into consideration foremost that although the technology behind Internet gaming is relatively new, the legal and policy issues underlying this important discussion are familiar ones. The fact is that there is a mature, effective gaming regulatory structure already in place and functioning. It is a structure that is consistent with core principles of federal Indian policy and one that recognizes the political status of tribal governments within the Constitutional framework of our Nation.

In IGRA, Congress established a unique system of shared regulatory responsibilities among the Federal Government, the states, and tribal governments, but designated tribal governments as the primary regulators of tribal gaming on Indian lands. To carry out the Federal Government's responsibilities in this structure, Congress created the NIGC, an independent federal regulatory agency within the Department of the Interior.

The NIGC's core mission is to provide federal civil regulatory oversight in order to shield Indian tribes from organized crime and other corrupting influences; ensure that Indian tribes are the primary beneficiaries of gaming revenue; and assure that gaming is conducted fairly and honestly by both operators and players. To that end, the NIGC has been vested with specific oversight powers and responsibilities under IGRA, including the authority to promulgate regulations and take enforcement actions.

Under current law, the respective roles of the NIGC and tribal governments are thus clearly defined and, as noted, consistent with well-established principles of federal Indian policy. It is a system that works and should be reflected in any new legislation pertaining to Internet gaming by tribal governments. Any legislation that would operate to bifurcate federal regulatory oversight responsibilities between the NIGC and another federal agency should be avoided as it would create uncertainties; increase the potential for inter-agency conflict; and subject tribal governments to oversight by federal agency personnel inexperienced in Indian Affairs, Indian law and policy, the federal-Indian relationship, and the regulation of gaming. Having two regulatory agencies regulating essentially the same functions would be redundant and problematic.

The NIGC, on the other hand, has nearly two decades of gaming regulatory experience, and its members and the staff understand the unique constitutional status of Indian tribes as sovereigns as well as the responsibilities associated with the special government-to-government relationship between tribal governments and the United States. Since the appointment of its first Chairman in 1993, the NIGC has grown considerably in size, scope, and sophistication. In October 1993, the NIGC had a staff of 27 and was responsible for overseeing 200 gaming operations operated by an estimated 175 tribal governments. The NIGC's staff now consists of over 120 employees who oversee an industry comprised of approximately 240 tribal governments operating over 420 tribal gaming operations in 28 states. The NIGC currently has field investigators operating out of seven regional offices and three satellite offices who work in conjunction with tribal gaming regulatory agencies in rendering technical assistance to tribal gaming operators. As a result, no other federal agency has achieved a comparable level of understanding in the tribal gaming context or possesses such experience.

There is no question that the NIGC is the ideal federal agency candidate to be assigned administrative jurisdiction over and implementation of any new legislation related to tribal Internet gaming. Besides its experience and longstanding relationships with tribal governments, particularly tribal gaming regulatory agencies, it is the only federal agency that possesses the regulatory infrastructure and tools to quickly and efficiently assume a gaming regulatory oversight role in relation to tribal Internet gaming.

The fact is that it takes years if not decades to establish a well-functioning regulatory agency. A new agency must assemble a capable staff, promulgate rules and regulations, meet all legal requirements applicable to all federal agencies, and commence operation. The NIGC's experiences during the first years of its formation are instructive in this regard. From the time the NIGC was first established by IGRA in 1988, it took nearly three years to appoint the first Chairman and assemble a skeleton staff, and another two years after that for the first set of regulations to become effective. Thus, it took nearly five years for the NIGC to actually begin carrying out its regulatory responsibilities. A similar delay in staffing an entire agency and ''gearing up'' the agency to begin regulating could prove disastrous for tribal governments and place them at a competitive disadvantage relative to non-tribal operators who are forging ahead under new state laws.

Although the regulation of Internet gaming will inevitably raise new regulatory and enforcement concerns, the NIGC possesses the necessary procedures and tools for monitoring and enforcing compliance with applicable gaming laws and regulations. The NIGC has already developed the institutional infrastructure for carrying out investigations, initiating enforcement actions, conducting hearings, and adjudicating appeals. It would be a relatively simple matter for the NIGC to add the technical expertise required to oversee the implementation of a tribal Internet gaming statute. Hence, the NIGC would not be hindered by a long start-up time or the kinds of delays involved in the formation of new agencies.

In addition, a key difference between the NIGC and other federal agencies is the NIGC's status as an independent regulatory agency. Independent regulatory agencies are generally charged with "independence" from other parts of the Executive Branch and are designed to enhance balance, provider greater stability, and mitigate the potential for sudden changes or reversals in agency policy likely to produce unnecessary or exceptionally severe economic harm to the regulated industry.

In establishing the NIGC as an independent regulatory agency, Congress intended to cloak the NIGC with the necessary independence and flexibility to work closely and freely with tribal governments in assuring the proper regulation of tribal gaming. Congress understood that insulation from external political influences would be critical to the successful implementation of the NIGC's regulatory oversight program. Any legislation that assigns regulatory oversight of tribal Internet gaming to a federal agency other than the NIGC would deprive tribal governments of the intended benefits of regulatory continuity and stability, and subject tribal governments to oversight by a federal agency that may be particularly vulnerable to abrupt changes in leadership, policy, resources, and organization.

In closing, I would note that what is most important is ensuring that the successes and investments that tribal governments have made in the gaming arena are not compromised. Nor should the Congress enact legislation that would place tribal governments at a competitive disadvantage by delaying tribal entry into the Internet gaming market. Sound regulatory institutions are well-established at both the federal and tribal levels of government and capable of performing regulatory functions in relation to Internet gaming. It would be neither cost-effective nor practical to re-invent new agencies when there are experienced and capable institutions currently in place to carry out important regulatory functions.

Thank you again for the opportunity to participate in this hearing. I am happy to answer any questions that you may have for me.

The CHAIRMAN. Thank you very much, Ms. Homer.

Mr. Porter, would you please proceed with your statement?

STATEMENT OF HON. JON C. PORTER, FORMER CONGRESSMAN; PRESIDENT, PORTER GORDON SILVER COMMUNICATIONS

Mr. PORTER. Thank you, Mr. Chairman. It is an honor for me to be here today. To you and certainly other Senators, my former colleague, Senator Udall, it is good to see you today. And to all of the Tribal leaders that are here today. I think it is an important day for America and for all those especially interested in Internet gaming.

I also want to say thank you to all your friends and family from Hawaii that visit Las Vegas. We want to continue that and we certainly do appreciate the customers that help support our economy.

Quickly, again, my name is Jon Porter. I served as a city councilman, a mayor, a State senator, most recently as an honored member of the U.S. Congress. I also had my own business for years. But I also believe that those combined give me a unique perspective to speak today. And for full disclosure, I do officially represent the Poker Players Alliance, 1.2 million members across the Country, although I am not speaking today on behalf of the PPA. I also represent numerous international gaming companies, not on a Federal level, but in a State arena; also a number of Tribal nations as well.

But today I was invited to speak, and I do appreciate that, and I want to applaud you and the Committee for addressing a very controversial but very important issue, and very timely. In essence, it is a game race played in interactive space, and I think it is critical for your involvement and your leadership.

I would like to give you a little bit of my Las Vegas political perspective. Many times I say I am from the State of Las Vegas, because sometimes people understand that better than some of the smaller communities. But look back at the history of Las Vegas. Just go back 50 years. In the early years we had some questionable ownership and minimal regulations and rules, and I like to say that our success, not unlike the success of the Tribal Nations, have been based upon some of the strongest regulatory rules and regulations and enforcement in the world. And I will say that again: some of the most difficult and the most strict rules and regulations in the world are placed upon gaming institutions, from the Tribal to the non-Tribal.

In fact, this is an exaggeration, but if you were to apply for a gaming license, the gaming control board may well go back to your grade school. So I suggest, if you are prepared, to make sure that you do your homework individually.

Also, part of Las Vegas' success is that we have been highly competitive with each other. Now, we certainly don't always agree in Las Vegas, but we are competitors. But we also come together when there are key issues, as does the Tribal Nation that impact their business.

So one of our successes has been the ability to work together.

Now, as you know, we have fought Federal regulation for years in the community of Las Vegas, in the early 1990s. We wanted to make sure that we could, in fact, use our gaming and regulatory body to make sure that our industry was certainly doing the right thing at the right time with the right people.

But my experience shows that I think there is a lot of parallel today between the Tribal Nations and the non-Tribal Nations. In early 2000, I can remember, in the Nevada State Senate, when we passed some of the first Internet gaming legislation, that was the beginning.

But over the next 12 years, and 6 years of that as a member of Congress, even the Las Vegas community wasn't quite sure what it wanted to do. I remember days when different gaming institutions would come into my office, and one day they would be for Internet gaming and one day they wouldn't be against it and they would be supportive. But I will tell you there has been a chance. Certainly not every gaming institution in Nevada supports Internet gaming, but we have had denial within our industry; we have had resistance; we have had acceptance. In fact, millions have been spent over the last 12 years.

Also, let me note a key issue, and my friend, Ms. Homer mentioned, acceptance of Internet for business is paramount, whether you are in the widget business or you are in the gaming business. You can use records and newspapers as an example of those that did not rush into the arena.

But I think what is paramount today is what one of the real issues is, and it is not really non-Tribal and Tribal conflict; I think the real question you are going to need to address is lotteries, eventually. Of course, I support poker only because I believe it is a game of skill, not a game of chance. But there are other interests besides Tribal and non-Tribal, because I believe we are very close in understanding, and we have worked together for years. But when we look at the lottery interests, many of them want to use a scratch card, which enters us into slot machines, and I think that debate should be for another day. Also, I believe that that would create an unfair competition for the Tribes and the non-Tribal companies.

So, in essence, I would like to cover, just before I conclude, a few constructive suggestions for my friends in the Tribal Nation.

Not unlike the non-Tribal, as you are moving forward into the Internet, and I encourage that companies do that and the Tribes, the big companies, the larger Tribes will have the resources to be engaged. There are hundreds of gaming institutions, Tribal and non-Tribal, around the Country; they are not all going to be able to be in the business. I encourage there be partnering in the Tribal Nation between non-Tribal Nation, as it is happening today successfully with Las Vegas properties. But also you could, as an industry and as a Nation, create a Tribal consortium dot com where a lot of the small groups could get together. It is an invaluable tool for economic.

Mr. Chairman, in closing, I think, number one, paramount, beyond the Tribes, beyond the non-traditional, and the non-Tribes, what is paramount is the safety and security of our families and kids that have access to the Internet, and I believe that the Tribal Nation, I believe that the non-Tribal, and certainly the lotteries want to make sure, first and foremost, children and families are taken care of.

We, and I, certainly support strong regulations. But to do nothing I think would be condoning the continuing of an abuse of the American people. There are 1,700 to 2,000 Internet sites around the world. I believe that the U.S. Senate and the U.S. House of Representatives must take action based upon the DOJ ruling that now everything appears to be legal except for sports betting.

So with that I again thank you very much. I know my time has expired. I look forward to working with you, your staff, and other members of the Senate, and I am indeed honored to be here today. Thank you very much.

[The prepared statement of Mr. Porter follows:]

PREPARED STATEMENT OF HON. JON C. PORTER, FORMER CONGRESSMAN; PRESIDENT, PORTER GORDON SILVER COMMUNICATIONS

Chairman Akaka and Members of the Committee, I am pleased to have this opportunity to testify before you today on the topic of regulation of tribal gaming, both on the Internet as well as traditional brick-and-mortar casinos. My past experience gives me a unique perspective due to my time as a mayor from suburban Las Vegas, Nevada State Senator, and as a Member of Congress from Nevada's 3rd Congressional District. At each level of government, I've either voted on gaming regulation or helped implemented it.

Today, I am the President of Porter Gordon Silver Communications, a full-service, bi-partisan government affairs and business consulting firm. With offices in Reno, Las Vegas, Carson City, Washington, D.C. and Phoenix, we offer advice and representation for our clients at the federal, state and local levels of government. We are also affiliated with Gordon Silver, one of the largest law firms in Nevada with a prominent gaming practice.

My current work is also relevant to today's discussion. I have numerous clients with Internet gaming interests including the Poker Players Alliance, an organization of 1.2 million American poker players, whom I am registered to represent at federal level, as well as multiple Nevada casinos and international online gaming companies, which doesn't include federal representation. I also consult on behalf of tribal interests outside of the gaming world. However, I would like to state that my thoughts today are my own and do not speak on behalf of any clients.

I've often described the Las Vegas of 50 years ago as the Wild West. There was little oversight, few regulations or regulatory bodies, and questionable casino ownership. Fast forward to today and you now see Vegas as the gold standard in gaming regulation. We have some of the most stringent licensing standards and toughest enforcement mechanisms. Right now, Mr. Chairman, if you were to apply for a gaming license in Las Vegas, you would be required to submit detailed personal history and financial information and be prepared to deliver five years of bank statements, credit card and brokerage statements, copies of contracts, deeds and titles to all assets, a list and summary of any litigation and such other information as contained in an application form. Further, gaming investigators will spend from four to six months in their review at a cost that ranges anywhere from $40,000 to over $1 million, depending upon history of the applicant and the complexity of the information provided, all of which is to be paid by the applicant. Needless to say, there is a strict application process.

This Nevada story parallels how Internet poker operates today. With the lack of federal regulation, online poker players are forced to play on their choice of over 1,700 foreign-based websites with little or no consumer protections and no oversight from federal regulators. There is no guarantee that the cards you see are truly random, or that multiple sites aren't colluding to take advantage of the player, that the person "sitting" next to you is actually a person and not a bot designed to win in the long run, or even that you'll have access to your money when you choose to cash out. Americans are not going to stop playing poker on the Internet, Mr. Chairman, that's the reality, so we need to view it as our responsibility to provide them a safe environment to play. We need to move from the Wild West of Internet gaming to current Las Vegas-style oversight.

It's clear that any industry which fails to embrace the Internet is doomed to failure. Think of the struggles that newspapers have been going through, or how long it took the recording industry to effectively sell digital music. Gaming is no different. It has already become extremely popular as an online activity, yet the Federal Government has refused to keep up with the times. It is my opinion that the time is now for the Congress and the Administration to bring laws and regulations into the 21st century by licensing and regulating online poker so those Americans playing today can know that they won't be taken advantage of.

My home state of Nevada is now a great example of how, historically, opposition to Internet poker was the knee-jerk reaction, yet the current times make it inevitable to embrace the benefits of online play. It wasn't long ago when I was taking meetings with brick-and-mortar Vegas casinos who would tell me that if I voted to regulate and license online poker, commercial casinos as we knew them would go bankrupt. Fast-forward a few years to where Nevada now has laws that allow intrastate Internet poker and already issued the first few licenses to accept online wagers, contingent on federal action. My point is that through working together and realizing the benefits that the Internet brings, operators and consumers will be much better off.

Now, more to the point of this hearing, how does the regulation of Internet gaming intersect with tribal interests. According to Wikipedia, there are 555 federally-recognized Indian tribes, and according to the NIGC, there are over 200 tribes engaged in some form of gaming. Moreover, there are roughly 445 non-tribal land-based or riverboat casinos within the US. No one reasonably believes that the U.S. market for Internet poker will support hundreds or even dozens of free-standing poker sites, and even many existing gaming facilities are unlikely to have the resources to launch their own free-standing Internet poker site. However, as I will discuss in a minute, there are numerous commercial opportunities for tribes and commercial casinos that can help them embrace the Internet to market their casinos and have a new channel of distribution to their customers without creating any cannibalization to their brick-and-mortar businesses. The critical ingredient for a successful Internet poker site is liquidity—having the critical mass of players such that any player can find the game they want, at the stakes they want, and at the time they want.

While no one can say for sure what the market would look like if H.R. 2366 or similar legislation is enacted, from the experience in Europe, we can surmise that there will be several ways in which tribes could profitably participate in the market other than simply as a free-standing licensee.

Many gaming tribes already have an established regional base of brick-and-mortar players who frequent their casinos. They could launch their own Internet sites and market to their brick-and-mortar players. For tribes without brick and mortar facilities, they could possibly partner in a consortium relationship with tribes who have casinos to increase the market share. Under this scenario, an existing gaming tribe could launch a poker site that could be utilized by other tribes where one played directly from the site and players would be actually playing on the lead tribal casino's software in a poker room where they are networked with other players who are also playing on the site. Indeed, if all, or a large swath of Indian country got together and launched shared sites, it could conceivably dominate the marketplace. Each tribe would have a URL of a site under their name, and market it to their players, but all those players would be networked with players from other tribes' sites across the country. Such an operation could dwarf even the large branded Las Vegas companies.

I feel like there has also been a perception, particularly in 2010 and 2011, that this was a fight between commercial gaming and tribal gaming, and, to be sure, commercial gaming was far more supportive of poker licensing legislation than Indian Country was. That was before the Department of Justice reversed its position on the application of the Wire Act to non-sports betting.

Since that decision, state lotteries have been increasingly aggressive in trying to get onto the Internet, providing traditional drawing tickets, but also providing other Internet games, including virtual scratch-off tickets that make computers function like slot machines. The vast majority of revenue for tribal gaming comes from slot machines, and that is because slot machines are relatively scarce on non-tribal land. If, however, you have state lotteries effectively turning every computer in the state into a potential slot machine, the competitive effect on tribal gaming is obvious. States like Delaware, Maryland, Illinois, Massachusetts and Georgia are already taking steps to take their lotteries online, and if they succeed, then others are bound to follow. I don't think tribal or commercial gaming interests would object to state lotteries selling their traditional drawing tickets on the Internet, but tribal and commercial gaming interests have been pretty clear that they do not think online slot machines are in the interests of commercial gaming, tribal gaming, or gaming consumers, for that matter. Poker is a small part of their brick-and-mortar business and does not pose a threat. On the other hand, full scale casinos create many other economic and policy issues.

If states seek to expand their lotteries to provide slot machine play into everyone's homes, the threat to commercial and tribal gaming is obvious. I would expect that this outcome would be unacceptable to those concerned about the societal impacts of gaming as well. However, in the absence of some federal legislation setting the rules of the road for Internet gaming, that outcome is likely in many states. Most versions of federal Internet gaming or poker legislation would prevent this; H.R. 2366 would only allow Internet poker to be played on the Internet, with Internet slots and other games clearly illegal under federal law. The emerging fault line isn't commercial vs. tribal gaming, but traditional gaming operations versus lotteries.

In conclusion, the story of brick-and-mortar casino regulation is not so different than what we're now doing with Internet gaming. The debate we're having may seem arduous and contentious at times, but it is a discussion that needs to be happening. My experience in Nevada gives me great hope and, if history is any indication, I'm confident we will design a strong regulatory structure that protects the consumer, respects tribal concerns, and is in the best interests of everyone involved.

Thank you, Mr. Chairman, for allowing me to share my thoughts with the Committee today and I look forward to answering any questions you may have.

The CHAIRMAN. Thank you. Thank you very much, Mr. Porter, for your testimony.

Mr. Johnson, would you please proceed with your testimony?

STATEMENT OF GENE JOHNSON, SENIOR VICE PRESIDENT, MARKET RESEARCH AND ONLINE STUDIES, SPECTRUM GAMING GROUP

Mr. JOHNSON. The Honorable Mr. Porter is a tough act to follow, but thank you, Chairman and members of the Committee. My name is Gene Johnson. I am a representative of Spectrum Gaming Group, a gaming industry consultant.

My first involvement with Internet gambling began more than a decade ago, when offshore companies were seeking to better understand the U.S. gaming market and little regulation exists. Because the question of legality was never settled through clear legislation in this Country, the Internet gambling industry developed and flourished overseas, in a market where originally the majority of players and revenue were American. Today this is a $30 billion industry representing almost 9 percent of all the money spent by gamblers worldwide, and it finally appears to be coming back to its country of origin.

The DOJ opinion of December 23rd, 2011, has opened the door for State lotteries to pursue online lotto sales, and it is only a matter of time until scratch and social games also appear on the Internet. Online scratch games involving a series of symbols, where the win outcome is determined by the last symbol, will be virtually indistinguishable from a slot machine once they are placed on the Internet. And now it becomes necessary to examine how online gambling should occur and what needs to be done to safeguard players and assure that online games are conducted fairly and responsibly.

Tribal gaming has already developed successful regulatory institutions and processes to administer land-based gambling, but interactive wagering brings a whole new set of challenges. Just as with land-based gambling, regulatory authorities will have to put in place responsible gaming protections, which include identity and age verification, geo-location, and other know your customer, or KYC, measures.

KYC is usually accomplished through a rigorous registration process that requires documentation of age, residence, location, credit card, and financial institution information. This is supported by employment of specific identity verification tools at every logon. In addition, Tribal regulators will need to establish anti-fraud procedures to prevent collusion and money laundering or chip dumping taking place on the games. All of this will require significant investment in technology.

Tribal regulators will need to establish effective regulations and enforce penalties for non-compliance. They will also need to develop testing procedures for the online games, as well as procedures for auditing the payment systems. They should be prepared to assess online gaming vendors and, if necessary, conduct background checks into the company principals. Some of these offshore B2C operators took bets from U.S. citizens after UIGEA was passed in 2006 and probably should not be allowed to benefit from those actions.

Most importantly, Tribal regulators and operators will need to acquire personnel resources with experience in online gambling operations and educate internal staff to build the knowledge base required to administer and regulate the new online operations.

Problem gambling will be just as tough an issue as it is with land-based gambling today. Increased availability of gambling through the Internet opens the potential for greater abuse, although research to date shows similar rates of problem in pathological gambling between the online and the offline channel.

The good news here is that the Internet offers better tools for tracking problem gamblers and even identifying patterns of behavior that lead to problem gambling so that early intervention can take place. Because online betting provides a perfect history of each player's gambling transactions, there is ample data available to profile normative gambling behavior, as well as abnormal gambling behavior. But the lesson to take from Europe is that problem gambling solutions, such as self-exclusion, need to be approached comprehensively on the Internet and not on a site-by-site basis.

While Internet gambling does present unique challenges, essentially it constitutes simply another channel for delivering the entertainment experience of responsible gaming. European operators have already established strong regulatory and KYC procedures that can be used as a model for U.S. operators, whether Tribal, commercial, or State lottery based. Spectrum believes that Internet gambling will develop in the U.S. differently from the European model and will be tied more closely to established land-based brands which can offer tangible player rewards and amenities.

Indian gaming is a major part of the land-based gambling industry, generating almost as much revenue as all the U.S. commercial casinos, and Tribal authorities will be expected to regulate online gambling just as effectively as they do bricks and mortar casinos.

That concludes my remarks. Thank you, members of the Committee.

[The prepared statement of Mr. Johnson follows:]

PREPARED STATEMENT OF GENE JOHNSON, SENIOR VICE PRESIDENT, MARKET RESEARCH AND ONLINE STUDIES, SPECTRUM GAMING GROUP

Thank you for providing this opportunity to address the committee on a subject in which I have extensive background.

My first involvement with Internet gambling was more than a decade ago when offshore companies were seeking to better understand the U.S. gaming market. Because the question of legality was never settled through clear legislation in this country, the Internet gambling industry developed and flourished overseas in a market where originally the majority of players (and revenue) were American. Today this is a $30 billion dollar industry representing almost 9 percent of all the money spent by gamblers worldwide last year.[1] Finally it appears that Internet gambling may be returning to its country of origin.

The Department of Justice opinion of December 23, 2011 has opened the door for state lotteries to pursue online lotto sales and it is only a matter of time until scratch and social games also appear on the Internet. Online scratch games, involving a series of symbols with the win outcome determined by the last symbol, will be virtually indistinguishable from a slot machine once placed on the Internet. Now that the prospect of legalized Internet gambling returning to the U.S. is has grown more probable, it becomes necessary to carefully examine how that should occur and what needs to be done to safeguard players and assure that online games are conducted fairly and responsibly—in short, the regulation of online gambling.

Tribal gaming has already developed successful regulatory institutions and processes to administer land-based gaming but interactive wagering brings a new set

---

[1] 2011 data set, H2 Gambling Capital.

of challenges which must also be addressed. Just as with land-based gaming, regulatory authorities will have to put in place responsible gaming protections which include identity and age verification, geo-location, and other "know your customer" (KYC) measures. KYC is usually accomplished through a rigorous registration procedure that requires documentation of age, residence, location, credit card and financial institution information. This is supported by the employment of specific identity verification tools at every logon. In addition tribal regulators will need to establish anti-fraud procedures to prevent collusion or money laundering (chip dumping) taking place on the games. All of this will require significant investment in technology.

Tribal regulators will need to establish effective regulations and enforce penalties for non-compliance. They will also need to develop testing procedures for the online games, as well as procedures for auditing the payment systems for Internet wagering sites. They should be prepared to assess online gaming vendors and if necessary conduct background checks into the company principals. Some of these offshore B2C operators took bets from US citizens after UIGEA was passed in 2006 and probably should not be allowed to profit from those actions.

Most importantly, tribal gaming regulators and operators will need to acquire resources with experience in current online gambling operations and educate internal staff to build the knowledge base required to administer and regulate the new online operations.

Problem gambling will be just as tough an issue as it is with land-based gaming. Increased availability of gambling through the Internet opens the potential for greater abuse, although research to date shows similar rates of problem and pathological gambling between the online and "offline" channels. The good news here is that Internet operations offer better tools for tracking problem gamblers, and even identifying patterns of behavior that lead to problem gambling so that early intervention can take place. Because online betting provides a perfect history of each player's gambling history, there is ample data available to profile normative gambling as well as abnormal gambling behavior. One lesson to take from Europe is that problem gambling solutions such as self-exclusion need to be approached comprehensively on the Internet and not on a site by site basis.

While Internet gambling does present unique challenges, essentially it constitutes simply another channel for delivering the entertainment experience of responsible gaming. European operators have already established strong regulatory and KYC procedures which can be used as a model for U.S. operations, whether tribal, commercial, or state lottery based. Spectrum believes that Internet gambling will develop in the U.S. differently from the European model and be tied more closely to established land-based brands which can offer tangible player rewards and amenities. Indian gaming is a major part of the land-based gambling industry, generating almost as much revenue as all U.S. commercial casinos, and tribal authorities will be expected to regulate online gaming just as effectively as it does bricks and mortar casinos.

Thank you.

The CHAIRMAN. Thank you. Thank you very much, Mr. Johnson, for your testimony.

Mr. Hummingbird, your organization is made up of Tribal regulators. Has your organization looked at the Internet game issue, or have individual members taken any steps to ensure Tribes are ready to participate should Federal legislation be enacted?

Mr. HUMMINGBIRD. Thank you, Mr. Chairman. The National Tribal Gaming Commissioners and Regulators have itself looked into this possibility on the avenue of providing training and education to Tribes and Tribal regulators, that is to say, getting them informed and getting them prepared for any eventuality for Internet gaming. I know that there are Tribes out there across the Country that have been proactively researching and drafting and looking at ways to take advantage of an opportunity should that come their way, but at this point I believe everybody is kind of waiting for whatever legislation may come down, because that is going to drastically impact the regulations and the ordinances that they may draft.

The CHAIRMAN. Ms. Homer, one of the issues that would severely limit a Tribe's ability to participate in or regulate Internet gaming centers around jurisdictional issues and how Indian lands would be treated. The question is what is your view on how Tribal lands should be taken into account in any Federal legislation?

Ms. HOMER. Well, I think that it is appropriate for there to be a strong regulatory presence by the Tribe over any Internet gaming that would entail locating the gaming equipment, locating the gaming system on the reservation, and subject to Federal and Tribal oversight. With regard to the market, however, I think that it would prove a terrible injustice to the Tribes if they were to be limited to Internet gaming that is initiated on the reservation. I think that it is only fair to, we are dealing with a borderless situation now, to allow Tribes to participate in the marketplace, whether it be the U.S. or a larger marketplace. The Tribes should be able to do that as long as they have their regulatory controls situated where they can actually be in control of it.

The CHAIRMAN. Congressman Porter, can you elaborate further on why you believe online gaming should be limited to poker only?

Mr. PORTER. Thank you, Mr. Chairman. First, let me highly encourage all the Tribal Nations to engage and be prepared, because something will be happening, it has to happen.

To answer your question, without getting into all the details of the difference between different types of gaming, but with poker, a poker player plays against another or with another poker player; whereas, the house in that case, whether it be a bricks and mortar, Tribal, non-Tribal, will normally receive some type of a fee, but they are not engaged in playing as a poker player against the house.

The advantage to poker only is, from a regulatory perspective, I really believe that it is a game of skill, and I can assure you, since I never win, I promise you it is a game of skill that I don't have; whereas, when you play a slot machine or some other form of casino game, you are technically playing against the house and the odds of the house, and a lot of times the house wins.

But I firmly believe that with the poker player, and, again, I work with close to a million, that it is certainly a game of skill; whereas, other games are a game of chance. And we want to make sure it is player-to-player and not player to some unknown site somewhere in the world, where we can't control what is happening within that database.

The CHAIRMAN. Thank you for that response.

Mr. Johnson, in your testimony you note that Indian gaming is a major part of the land-based gambling industry, generating nearly as much revenue as all U.S. commercial gaming. Do you see any reason why Tribes should be prohibited from entering the online gaming market at the same time as those other gaming interests?

Mr. JOHNSON. That is a great question. No, I do not see any reason why the Tribes should be prohibited. And in States where there are no commercial or Tribal gaming interests, it is very likely that the State lottery will seek to acquire a monopoly on online gaming activities. But the Tribes have demonstrated the social benefits of land-based Tribal gaming and I think it would only help to enhance their operations and their charitable operations, what they do to support their own people and to make themselves independent of Federal assistance. So by all means they deserve an equal place at the table as commercial gaming and State lotteries would.

The CHAIRMAN. Thank you very much, Mr. Johnson.

Mr. Hummingbird and Ms. Homer, this is to both of you. Does Congress need to amend IGRA or revise any existing Tribal-State compacts for Tribes to participate in online gaming?

Ms. HOMER. Thank you.

That is a really good question, Senator, and I think that it would be very unwise to undo any Tribal gaming compacts. The nice thing about Tribal gaming compacts is that they are a bargain between the States and the Tribes, and they are subject to renegotiation or they are subject to discussion and agreement and accord between the parties here. I don't see that need to reopen the Indian Gaming Regulatory Act and to amend the Indian Gaming Regulatory Act, per se.

I think that it is quite possible to have an independent piece of legislation or to create a new title to the larger Internet gaming legislation that is, or any larger Internet gaming legislation that is being considered that would be specific to Tribal Governments. There is no reason why the NIGC couldn't be assigned administrative jurisdiction over two separate statutes. Federal agencies are assigned multiple statutes to administer all the time. So I don't think we would have to disturb IGRA in order to have a viable quality Tribal Internet gaming bill.

The CHAIRMAN. Mr. Hummingbird?

Mr. HUMMINGBIRD. Thank you, Mr. Chairman. I would echo Elizabeth's comments in the sense that I do not believe it would be necessary to amend IGRA. I think any Federal legislation that we would be looking at would need to either be viewed as diminishing its impact on any Tribal-State impacts that are out there, if not protecting their contents outright. I think it would be in the best interest of Tribes to provide a protection for the existing compacts without having to amend IGRA.

The CHAIRMAN. Thank you. Thank you very much.

Mr. Porter, Congressman Porter, in your testimony you note the historic knee jerk reaction against online gaming. In your view, can the benefits that Nevada brick and mortar casinos now foresee in online play be shared and replicated by Tribal gaming operators?

Mr. PORTER. Thank you, Mr. Chairman. I certainly would agree, but I also think it is vice versa; I think that we can learn from each other. As I mentioned in my testimony, I think one of the bigger problems is the bigger picture is extending into a scratch card and to slot machines. But I certainly that as we have done as a community with the Tribal Nation for the last 20 years, we have worked together and, again, have created some of the toughest regulations in the world on ourselves.

So I certainly think we have a lot to offer, but I also believe that the non-Tribal, our industry in Nevada, too, has a lot to offer. But that is why your conversations today with the Committee and other members gives us an opportunity to share some ideas. But they are also working together now, quite effectively, across the Country. So I think it is a team effort. We have a lot to give from both sides.

The CHAIRMAN. Mr. Johnson, do you think Tribes should be able to form Tribal consortiums to enhance their ability to participate in online gaming should Federal legislation be enacted?

Mr. JOHNSON. Thank you, Mr. Chairman. Again, I would say, without question, they should be. If you look at the history of the lottery industry, I believe it was 1962, there were no lotteries in the United States, and New Hampshire was the first, I believe, and it took years of litigation for lotteries to win the rights to have multiple State compacts, to have games that had a jackpot you could play across a number of States, specifically games like Megamillions and PowerBall.

When you look at online poker, small States such as Delaware, which has legalized Internet gambling, have very small populations and very little liquidity. Liquidity is the mass effect of having a number of players on the site and the ability to find a game within your price point at any time. Without liquidity, small States and small Tribes will suffer; it will be very difficult for them to gain traction in order to compete with commercial casinos and offshore operators. I think interTribal or interstate compacts are going to be essential.

The CHAIRMAN. Thank you very much. I want to tell this panel your responses have been helpful, coming from the experiences and the areas that you come from, and the parts of the Country that you come from really makes a difference, and we are trying to work together with the Tribes to bring about some of the what we might consider necessary values that can keep the industry successful and working well. So I want to thank you very, very much for your responses. You may receive some questions from members of the Committee that they may have.

So I want to thank our witnesses for participating in today's hearing. We have heard quite a bit today regarding regulation of Tribal gaming as it currently exists. We also have a lot to consider should Federal legislation be enacted that expands gaming in the United States.

As always, it is our job on the Committee to make sure Tribes achieve parity in any Federal legislation and to bring your voice to Congress, so I urge all of you to review the Tribal Online Gaming Act, the discussion draft, and provide comments so that you can make sure the Tribal voice is heard.

We will continue the dialogue on this issue and I encourage all of you to continue to work with this Committee. Again, thank you for being so patient and I want to wish all of you well in your endeavors, and we want to do the best we can to provide the best operation regulations that we can to all of you.

Before I really call for adjournment, I would ask the panel if they have any final comments they would like to make to the Committee.

Ms. Homer?

Ms. HOMER. Senator, I just want to thank you for your service to Indian Country during your tenure in the Senate. I know that you are looking at retiring, and we are going to miss you so very much, and your wisdom and your kindness and your compassion. So I just want to say thank you.

The CHAIRMAN. Thank you.

Congressman Porter?

Mr. PORTER. And I echo the same, Mr. Chairman. We appreciate your service.

But I heard something today quite consistently from some of the Tribal Nations, and that is that they are waiting to see what is going to happen, and even maybe from the regulatory standpoint. I would suggest, as a company that specializes in licensing, Porter Gordon Silver, I would highly encourage the Tribal Nations and the regulatory bodies get engaged quickly in this debate from creating their own regulations and being a part of this.

One thing that Nevada has done, of course, I am most slightly biased, coming from Las Vegas, but one thing Nevada has done in anticipating that this may happen soon, we have passed landmark legislation to prepare our industry for this global Internet. And I know other States have and I, of course, am not here from the other States, but a lot of States are moving and preparing. I would highly encourage, with your leadership and the Committee, that the Tribal Nations be prepared and not wait, because I feel it is a responsibility of Congress to do something and the Senate to protect families, and I think they should be prepared or they will miss the opportunity.

So, again, thank you, Mr. Chairman. It is an honor to be here.

The CHAIRMAN. Thank you.

Mr. Johnson?

Mr. JOHNSON. I would just like to expand on the earlier question you asked about the interTribal networks. I mentioned the example of Delaware being a small State. You can be sure that the States, the State lotteries, when they go online, they will ban together in multi-State networks, it is only a matter of time; and the Tribes should look to do that as well.

And, once again, thank you, sincere thanks for the invitation to speak before the Committee.

The CHAIRMAN. Thank you very much for being here.

Mr. Hummingbird.

Mr. HUMMINGBIRD. Thank you, Mr. Chairman. I too want to express my appreciation for your leadership on this Committee. I think you have done an honorable job and have represented Indian Country and Native peoples very well.

I do want to dovetail into something that Mr. Porter had just spoken of, and it is a message that I have been advocating every chance I can get, and I don't think there is a better chance I can get than this one today, but that is for Tribes to be prepared, to be aware, and to be active; and those three simple phrases contain a lot of activity that Tribes will be need to be cognizant of. We have to be prepared for what eventuality is coming.

The Tribal Online Gaming Act is something that is going to be of much interest to Tribes in the very near future. But we also have to be aware of everything surrounding this particular issue, and it is something that I have encouraged our Tribal leadership and I encourage the elected leadership at the Senate and the House side to continue in dialogue such as what we had today, bringing those individuals to the table that can provide a more round view of the issue at hand, because it is very important to get this particular item right the first time out from the gate so that we can have something that is going to be a viable option and hopefully complement the economic success that Tribes have garnered through gaming up to this time.

So thank you for this hearing. I hope we have the opportunity to speak on future occasions and to advance the cause of regulation for Indian gaming. Thank you.

The CHAIRMAN. Thank you very much, all of you on this panel. I want to say mahalo, thank you very much. Without question, let's continue to work together on this.

This hearing is adjourned.

[Whereupon, at 4:30 p.m., the Committee was adjourned.]

APPENDIX

PREPARED STATEMENT OF GRANT W. EVE, CPA, CFE, PARTNER, JOSEPH EVE

Chairman Akaka and Members of the Committee, for the record my name is Grant Eve, CPA, a partner with the regional CPA firm of JOSEPH EVE. I am writing this to be submitted to the records for the United States Senate Committee on Indian Affairs Oversight Hearing on Regulation of Tribal Gaming: From Brick and Mortar to the Internet that was held on July 26, 2012. This is to add some clarification on the National Indian Gaming Commission (Commission) Minimum Internal Control Standards Agreed Upon Procedures (NIGC MICS AUP) that was discussed in the question and answer section of NIGC Chairwoman Tracie Stevens and Senator Barrasso, Senator Franken, and Senator Udall.

NIGC Minimum Internal Control Standards 542.3(f) (1) states that an independent certified public accountant (CPA) shall be engaged to perform "Agreed-Upon-Procedures" to verify that the gaming operation is in compliance with the minimum internal control standards (MICS) set forth in this part or a Tribally approved variance thereto that has received Commission concurrence. The CPA shall report each event and procedure discovered by or brought to the CPA's attention that the CPA believes does not satisfy the minimum standards or Tribally approved variance that has received Commission concurrence. The "Agreed-Upon Procedures" may be performed in conjunction with the annual audit. The CPA shall report its findings to the Tribe, Tribal gaming regulatory authority, and management. The Tribe shall submit two copies of the report to the Commission within 120 days of the gaming operation's fiscal year end. This regulation is intended to communicate the Commission's position on the minimum agreed-upon procedures to be performed by the CPA. Throughout these regulations, the CPA's engagement and reporting are based on Statements on Standards for Attestation Engagements (SSAEs) in effect as of December 31, 2003, specifically SSAE 10 ("Revision and Recodification Agreed-Upon Procedures Engagements."). If future revisions are made to the SSAEs or new SSAEs are adopted that are applicable to this type of engagement, the CPA is to comply with any new or revised professional standards in conducting engagements pursuant to these regulations and the issuance of the agreed-upon procedures report.

Our CPA firm, JOSEPH EVE, performs several tribal casino financial statement audits and MICS AUP procedures each year. A tribal casino could be subject to as many as 15 individual MICS checklists. The gaming machine MICS checklist has 192 questions. A casino could be out of compliance with a one or two of the 192 questions and a "finding" is written up for each question where the casino is out of compliance. Materiality is not a consideration when performing the NIGC MICS AUP procedures as it is in a financial statement audit. It is our professional opinion that it is very difficult to state whether a casino that is out of compliance with one or two questions subjects either the casino or the customers to an undue risk.

Senator Udall requested to know what percentages of tribes are out of compliance with the NIGC MICS AUP. In our opinion, with the NIGC MICS AUP, it would be difficult to measure whether the tribe is in or out of compliance, as a whole. In our experience, almost all gaming operations have some non-compliance issues that are identified in conjunction with the NIGC MICS AUP procedures. As the NIGC MICS are cumbrous, some internal controls are more stringent that others, so therefore, it would be very challenging to say after a certain number of findings, a tribe is out of compliance as a whole. The CPA firm that is completing AUP procedures must complete the CPA NIGC MICS compliance checklists or other comparable testing procedures. The checklists measure compliance on a sampling basis by performing walkthroughs, observations and substantive testing. The CPA completes separate checklists for each gaming revenue center, cage and credit, internal audit, surveillance, information technology and complimentary services or items.

In addition to the checklists, the CPA firm must complete one unannounced observation of each of the following: gaming machine coin drop, gaming machine currency acceptor drop, table games drop, gaming machine coin count, gaming machine currency acceptor drop, and table games count. For purposes of these procedures, "unannounced" means that no officers, directors, or employees are given advance information regarding the dates and times of such observations. This unannounced observation is an integral piece of the NIGC MICS AUP procedures. This can difficult to complete as a true unannounced observation if the CPA firm does not have tribal gaming experience and understand how the casino operates in conjunction with the tribal gaming regulatory authority.

Alternatively, at the discretion of the Tribe, the Tribe may engage an independent certified public accountant (CPA) to perform the testing, observations and procedures reflected in paragraphs (f)(1)(i), (ii), and (iii) of 542.3 utilizing the Tribal internal control standards adopted by the Tribal gaming regulatory authority or Tribally approved variance that has received Commission concurrence. Accordingly, the CPA will verify compliance by the gaming operation with the Tribal internal control standards. Should the Tribe elect this alternative, as a prerequisite, the CPA will compare the Tribal internal control standards to the MICS to ascertain whether the criteria set forth in the MICS or Commission approved variances are adequately addressed. The CPA may utilize personnel of the Tribal gaming regulatory authority to cross-reference the Tribal internal control standards to the MICS, provided the CPA performs a review of the Tribal gaming regulatory authority personnel's work and assumes complete responsibility for the proper completion of the work product. If a tribe decides to utilize these alternative procedures, based on their tribal internal control standards, it may not be comparing "apples to apples." The tribe may have more stringent internal controls as requested by tribal council, the gaming commission, or could be required in the state compact. Therefore, it would not be possible to state percentages that are in or out of compliance.

Other factors to consider while analyzing if a tribe is in or out of compliance with the NIGC MICS AUP procedures include:

- Whether the CPA firm relied on the internal auditors of the gaming operation
- When the unannounced observations took place
  - If the gaming operations year-end is 12/31 and the unannounced observation took place on 12/30, it would not be a true unannounced observation as management would be able to tell when the procedures were to take place using process of elimination.
- The experience of the CPA firm that conducts the audit and NIGC MICS AUP
- Whether the gaming operation continues to have repeat exceptions year after year

In closing, we would be happy to answer any questions the Senate Committee on Indian Affairs may have regarding this submission, tribal casino audit procedures, or procedures related to the NIGC MIC AUP engagements.

————

JOINT PREPARED STATEMENT OF KATHRYN R.L. RAND, J.D. AND STEVEN ANDREW LIGHT, PH.D., CO-DIRECTORS, INSTITUTE FOR THE STUDY OF TRIBAL GAMING LAW AND POLICY

We thank Chairman Akaka, Vice Chairman Barrasso, and the members of the U.S. Senate Committee on Indian Affairs for this opportunity to comment on the Discussion Draft of the Tribal Online Gaming Act (TOGA) of 2012 following the Committee's July 26, 2012 oversight hearing on the regulation of Indian gaming and online gaming. [1]

We co-direct the Institute for the Study of Tribal Gaming Law and Policy at the University of North Dakota, which provides legal and policy analysis and advances research and understanding of Indian gaming. Our comments and suggestions here are informed by sixteen years of research and interaction with those involved with Indian gaming.

We welcome this opportunity to contribute our views on how best to legislate in the area of Tribal Online Gaming in the context of the current Indian Gaming industry and the prospects for federal legalization of online gaming generally. In this statement, we focus on one key question—how best to ensure effective federal oversight and regulatory authority of Tribal Online Gaming—and also provide several more limited suggestions related to consistency and clarity in the TOGA.

---

[1] The analysis of tribal considerations for online gaming when Congress appeared poised to legislate in 2011 has been retained in Committee files. *See* Kathryn R.L. Rand & Steven Andrew Light, *Indian Gaming on the Internet: How the Indian Gaming Ethic Should Guide Tribes' Assessment of the Online Gaming Market*, 15 GAMING L. REV. 11 (2011): 681–691.

1. Tribal Online Gaming Oversight and Regulatory Authority

The TOGA calls for the U.S. Secretary of Commerce to oversee and regulate Tribal Online Gaming, with assistance from a new "Office of Tribal Online Gaming," headed by a Director within the Commerce Department.

We believe that assigning primary regulatory authority over Tribal Online Gaming to the Secretary of Commerce and a new office within the Commerce Department fails to take advantage of existing regulatory expertise and experience—namely the National Indian Gaming Commission (NIGC)—and creates a heightened risk of interagency inconsistency and inefficiency, hindering the TOGA's effectiveness. We therefore recommend that the NIGC be delegated primary regulatory authority over Tribal Online Gaming through the TOGA. To ensure efficiency and to guard against inconsistency among federal agencies charged with regulation of state and commercial online gaming, we suggest including a liaison mechanism between the NIGC and the Secretary of Commerce.

a. NIGC as Primary Regulator of Tribal Online Gaming

Since its establishment under the Indian Gaming Regulatory Act (IGRA) in 1988 as an independent regulatory agency, the NIGC has developed expertise in effective regulation of Indian gaming, including approval of tribal gaming ordinances and management contracts, oversight of tribal licensing of key employees and management officials, investigation and enforcement actions, and promulgation of regulations—all duties nearly identical to the regulatory functions set forth in the TOGA.

When Congress legalizes online gaming, it will require implementing effective regulation as immediately as possible. Given its current regulatory oversight of Indian gaming, the NIGC is uniquely situated to provide immediate, effective, and appropriately policy-driven oversight of Tribal Online Gaming.

The NIGC's operations have been informed by IGRA's policy goals of promoting tribal economic development, self-sufficiency, and strong tribal governments, alongside effective gaming regulation—exactly what the TOGA sets out in its policy goals. These policy goals in turn reflect the Federal Government's established trust obligation to tribes and the body of federal Indian law and policy.

The NIGC provides technical assistance to tribes in establishing and implementing effective tribal gaming commissions. For instance, the NIGC has developed a Model Tribal Gaming Ordinance, trained tribal regulators, and promulgated Minimum Internal Control Standards—all of which are essential for effective regulation and coordinated oversight, as well as facilitating strong tribal governments and tribal self-sufficiency. The NIGC also has worked to develop meaningful government-to-government relations with tribes and to facilitate effective intergovernmental relations among federal, state, and tribal officials. The NIGC's experience, expertise, and relationships with tribes have been built over more than two decades and reflect the dynamic nature of the Indian gaming industry and the obligations inherent in multi-jurisdictional oversight and regulation.

Primary regulatory authority over Tribal Online Gaming may be delegated to the NIGC through the TOGA, without any need to amend IGRA or other existing federal law. The scope of this regulatory authority should be clearly and expressly described in the TOGA to avoid any confusion about the extent of the NIGC's powers or overlap with regulation of Indian gaming under IGRA. *See, e.g., Colorado River Indian Tribes v. NIGC*, 466 F.3d 134 (D.C. Cir. 2006).

To allow the addition of appropriate regulatory capacity and online gaming expertise, the NIGC should receive appropriate additional funding, perhaps through the Tribal Online Gaming licensing process.

b. Coordination of Regulation of Tribal and Non-Tribal Online Gaming Through Liaison Mechanism

If regulation of non-Tribal Online Gaming is delegated to the Secretary of Commerce while the NIGC has primary regulatory authority over Tribal Online Gaming, it will be essential to appropriately coordinate regulation of online gaming generally. To take full advantage of the NIGC's existing expertise, coordinate effective federal regulation of all online gaming, and avoid interagency inconsistency in interpretation and implementation of the TOGA, we suggest incorporating a liaison mechanism.

While the TOGA provides for memoranda of agreement among the Secretary of Commerce, the NIGC Chair, and the Attorney General to ensure sharing of information, we suggest that more direct coordination is necessary. An example in the context of Indian gaming illustrates the potential pitfalls.

Inconsistency in the NIGC's and the Department of Justice's interpretations of the Johnson Act in the context of Class II machines resulted in extensive litigation and uncertainty. The NIGC classified certain machines as Class II devices, allowing tribes to operate them in the absence of a tribal-state compact, IGRA's requirement for Class III gaming. At the same time, the Justice Department threatened tribes with criminal prosecution under the Johnson Act for operating those Class II machines without a tribal-state compact. *See, e.g., United States v. 103 Electronic Gambling Devices*, 223 F.3d 1091 (9th Cir. 2000); *Seneca-Cayuga Tribe of Oklahoma v. NIGC*, 327 F.3d 1019 (10th Cir. 2003); *United States v. Santee Sioux Tribe of Nebraska*, 324 F.3d 607 (8th Cir. 2003). This interagency conflict resulted in costs both to tribes and the Federal Government and undermined effective and efficient regulation of Indian gaming.

Thus, we suggest a liaison mechanism to ensure effective communication among federal agencies and thus effective coordination of federal regulation of online gaming generally.

Such a liaison mechanism could focus mostly on communication, such as by convening a "Tribal Online Gaming Working Group," modeled after the Indian Gaming Working Group established in 2004 among the NIGC, the Federal Bureau of Investigation, the Department of the Interior Office of the Inspector General, the Internal Revenue Service Tribal Government Section, the Bureau of Indian Affairs Law Enforcement Services, the Department of the Treasury Financial Crimes Enforcement Network, and the United States Attorneys Subcommittee on Indian Matters. The Indian Gaming Working Group is intended to enhance cooperation between agencies, obtain commitment to undertake an active role in effective regulation, pool federal resources, coordinate regulatory roles and functions, and develop investigative strategies. A Tribal Online Gaming Working Group might similarly bring together the NIGC, the Secretary of Commerce, and the Justice Department.

Alternatively, a more structured approach that builds coordination into the NIGC's regulatory functions could include the appointment via the TOGA of additional NIGC Commissioners charged solely with participating in regulation of Tribal Online Gaming. For example, two Tribal Online Gaming Commissioners could be added to the NIGC, perhaps a tribal member with experience in gaming regulation (appointed by the Secretary of Commerce in consultation with the Secretary of the Interior and the Attorney General), and a member of the Commerce Department agency charged with regulation of non-Tribal Online Gaming (appointed in the same manner as required for appointment to the Commerce Department agency). The authority of these Tribal Online Gaming Commissioners would be limited to the regulation of Tribal Online Gaming under the TOGA. They would not have regulatory authority over Indian gaming under IGRA, and their appointment would not require amending IGRA. The NIGC, acting with the additional Tribal Online Gaming Commissioners, should have the regulatory powers set forth in the TOGA.

This format, with the addition of the Tribal Online Gaming Commissioners coupled with the expertise and experience of the NIGC, should result immediately and in the long term in the effective regulation of Tribal Online Gaming that is appropriately coordinated with the regulation of online gaming generally.

2. Other Suggestions Related to Definitions, Consistency, and Clarity

a. Definition of Tribal Online Gaming

The legal term "Tribal Online Gaming," should be used consistently throughout the bill. For instance, Section 4(1) references "Internet gaming" rather than Tribal Online Gaming. This type of inconsistency is more than a stylistic or semantic concern. The same way that "Indian gaming" is a legal term of art defined by and incorporated throughout IGRA, and both reflects and shapes the industry's legal, policy, and regulatory environment, Tribal Online Gaming should be distinct and used consistently as defined by the TOGA. The TOGA's definition of Tribal Online Gaming (Section 3(5)) should mirror the definition of state and commercial online gaming in federal legislation that authorizes such gaming. We also note that Section 13(b) purports to automatically amend the statutory definition of Tribal Online Gaming when and if states are allowed to conduct online gaming beyond poker. We suggest a cleaner way to achieve this might be through a definition that mirrors federal legalization of state online gaming. For instance: "The term 'Tribal Online Gaming' means gaming conducted over the Internet in accordance with this Act and extends to the same specific online games that federal law allows states to conduct."

b. Indian Lands

Though not included in the definitions section, the TOGA uses the term "tribal land" (*see* Section 6(g)(2)). The definition of this term is not clear, though we believe the intent is to mirror the "Indian lands" defined in IGRA as reservation lands or trust and restricted lands over which a tribe exercises governmental authority. As IGRA's definition of "Indian lands" and the Major Crimes Act's definition of "Indian country'' are the two most prevalent terms of art in federal law, we suggest using the term Indian lands with the same definition as appears in IGRA to avoid uncertainty, confusion, and litigation.

c. Inapplicability of IGRA

Similarly, to avoid litigation and uncertainty arising from confusion about how the TOGA and Tribal Online Gaming relate to Class II and Class III Indian gaming as defined by IGRA, we suggest clarifying that IGRA does not apply to Tribal Online Gaming, other than as expressly provided by the TOGA. In Section 12, we suggest adding the clear statement that no tribal-state compact is required for a tribe to conduct Tribal Online Gaming in compliance with the TOGA to avoid confusion with IGRA's requirement for Class III gaming.

d. Tribes as Primary Beneficiaries

We concur that the TOGA's policy goals, consistent with those of IGRA, remain principal goals of federal Indian policy, and align with the needs of tribal governments and communities. We therefore suggest considering whether tribes should be explicitly designated as the primary beneficiaries of Tribal Online Gaming, as required of Indian gaming under IGRA.

e. Revenue Sharing

Section 16 of the TOGA requires tribes participating in online gaming to pay one percent of gross gaming revenues (presumably, though not expressly, limited to Tribal Online Gaming revenues) into a fund that will be disbursed to tribes that choose not to conduct online gaming (''Indian tribes that have opted out of participation in tribal online lending [sic] . . .''). Though termed ''Revenue Sharing,'' this provision is modeled after California's Revenue Sharing Trust Fund (*see Rincon Band of Luiseno Mission Indians v. Schwarzenegger*, 602 F.3d 1019 (9th Cir. 2010)), rather than the more typical revenue-sharing agreements that have sprung from IGRA's tribal-state compact requirement for Class III gaming. We suggest that the goals of this provision could be achieved in ways that are more appropriately tailored to the purpose, and that do not cause further confusion about the limitations on revenue-sharing provisions in tribal-state compacts under IGRA.

We thank the Committee for its consideration of this statement at an important juncture for Indian gaming as well as for online gaming. We would be happy to answer any questions or elaborate on the suggestions we offer here, and to address any other issues related to Tribal Online Gaming that the Committee deems pertinent.

PREPARED STATEMENT OF HON. ROBERT ODAWI PORTER, PRESIDENT, SENECA NATION OF INDIANS

Introduction

Greetings. On behalf of the Seneca Nation of Indians (the ''Nation''), I submit the following preliminary comments to the Committee for its use as it shapes its draft legislation on tribal online gaming.

On-line gaming by off-shore operators is an inevitable and competitive participant in the market in which the Nation conducts its gaming activities. Some estimates indicate that in 2010, between 10 and 15 million people in the United States bet billions of dollars online, even though it was illegal for companies to offer real-money Internet gambling in the U.S. Americans will continue to bet online as long as there are sites they can access, and off-shore operators will always create sites Americans can access as long as there are billions of dollars to be made.

Indian nations, including the Seneca Nation of Indians, have closely monitored the growing competitive threat which Internet gambling poses to our brick and mortar casino operations. Yet each tribal nation has been relegated to the sidelines as various bills were introduced and considered in this and prior sessions of the Congress. These bills have thus far not been enacted because of the potentially broad impact they would have on Internet providers, states and segments of the gaming industry. But as proposed, these bills should not be enacted because they would breach treaties and other agreements between the United States and Indian nations like the Seneca Nation of Indians. Moreover, these bills would limit tribal participation or require unfairly restrictive conditions on tribal involvement. In all instances, the bills were developed without Indian tribes.

Our Nation commends the Committee for attempting to involve Indian nations in shaping a legislative alternative that responds to tribal concerns by drafting, and seeking tribal comment upon, the draft Tribal Online Gaming Act of 2012. However, as described more fully below, the Committee's draft bill does not adequately ensure that tribal rights and interests are protected. Perhaps this is due to the unfortunate fact that there was a complete lack of tribal consultation and participation in the drafting of the Committee's draft bill. At least for our part, the Nation had absolutely no inkling of what was to be in the Committee's draft bill until you circulated it. In addition, most of the draft bill is very similar, if not identical in several respects, to H.R. 2366, the Internet Gambling Prohibition, Poker Consumer Protection and Strengthening UIGEA Act of 2011 introduced during the 112th Congress.

What follows are a number of issues we have identified preliminarily in the Committee's draft bill which should be substantially revised.

Poker Only. We understand the Committee's apparent effort to constrain the proposed new online authority to the scope of gaming—poker only—currently rumored to be under consideration by the U.S. Congress. However, the Committee draft's definition of "tribal online gaming" is not as expansive as the "online gaming" definition found in H.R. 2366 and other previous bills which proposed to legalize Internet gambling facilities presumably to allow those facilities to offer other Class II type games in addition to poker. Indeed, many of the Internet gaming sites currently available include computer based games that mimic slot machines or video lottery games designated as Class II. A broader definition would facilitate a tribal nation's ability to adapt its Internet gambling site quickly to accommodate future online gaming that may be legalized for others by the Congress.

The draft legislation authorizes only online poker initially, but says that "[i]f subsequent federal law allows states to conduct online gaming in addition to online poker games, Indian tribes shall be offered the same right to conduct that online gaming." Instead, the bill should authorize an Indian nation to conduct all forms of online gaming from day one, rather than just poker, and rather than waiting for additional federal legislation. On the basis of the USDOJ's recent December 2011 Wire Act opinion, federal law does not appear to prohibit intrastate online gaming if authorized by state law. If states do pursue or allow intrastate online gaming and such gaming proves to be lucrative, additional federal legislation may never come and tribal nation gaming operators could be placed at a significant competitive disadvantage by this initial limitation to only poker.

As an aside, it should be noted that the draft bill contains one reference to the term "Internet gambling facility" (See Section 6 (d) (E) Safeguards Required of Licensee) and for consistency with the balance of the bill should be revised to read "tribal online gaming" facility, and in the same vein, the draft bill should include definitions of "significant vendor", "remote gaming equipment", "controlling interest" and "Bots".

Federal Oversight. The Committee's draft bill would establish federal guidelines to assure that there is consistency in the regulation of Internet gaming (online poker) and thereby avoid a patchwork of rules and regulations. The Nation believes a single, federal-wide regulatory regime may prove to be beneficial not only for customers but for law enforcement and the regulators, and help ensure fairer competition for tribal nations seeking to engage in online gaming.

Commerce Department. Designating the U.S. Commerce Department as the federal regulatory oversight agency for tribal online gaming is ill-advised and would be a significant mistake. The Commerce Department has only very limited experience working with Indian nations. It has no experience with gaming regulatory or enforcement activity or gaming policy. Consequently it would start out far behind and never catch up to the dynamic, fast-paced, and technologically-driven, worldwide competitive market. It will need to develop an infrastructure and expertise that will be subject to inherent bureaucratic obstacles frequently experienced by federal agencies. All of this federal "oversight" would result in delaying the entry of tribal operators into the online gaming market.

National Indian Gaming Commission. In contrast to the U.S. Commerce Department, the National Indian Gaming Commission (NIGC) with its existing tribal gaming expertise and experience, would provide a more ready and capable regulatory structure with which the United States could oversee and regulate tribal online gaming. The NIGC already has over twenty years' experience working with gaming tribes, it has already developed a data base of gaming sites and the lands that tribal nations govern. And it has a regulatory and training program in place, not just for the staff but for tribal leaders and employees. Even more compelling is the fact that the NIGC already has a system in place to conduct background investigations of gaming companies and principals. It works closely with the Federal Bureau of Investigations (FBI) to assist tribal nations in assessing criminal history information for background investigations. As an independent agency, the NIGC is exempt from time-consuming personnel policies relating to appointments and restrictive compensation requirements. As such, the NIGC is able to hire within weeks rather than the months other federal agencies normally take. Altogether, the NIGC's experience, expertise in Indian gaming regulation and established infrastructure make it the only federal agency that can step right in and take charge of tribal online gaming regulation and oversight.

Licensure Requirements. The licensing provisions of the draft bill include several scenarios in which tribal nations may conduct lawful online gaming, including in consortium with non-tribal entities (see below). Otherwise, we find generally acceptable the standards for licensure which are fairly restrictive and include safeguards to protect the consumer, to prevent minors from gambling, and to prevent fraud, money laundering and financing of terrorism.

Opt-In/Opt-Out. The time limit for a tribal nation to opt in or opt out should be revised to be distinct from the time limit for publication of the list of participating tribes. As drafted both events would occur simultaneously.

Location of Remote Gaming Equipment. The crucial language in the Committee's draft that references the location of remote gaming equipment is unclear (e.g., "if the requirement applies to all significant vendors or other entities").

Tribal Ordinances and Compliance with Other Federal Law. The Committee's draft bill requires a tribal nation seeking to operate an online gaming site to adopt a tribal ordinance in accordance with federal standards and in compliance with any other federal law. Does this mean the Interstate Wire Act of 1961, the Unlawful Internet Gambling Enforcement Act of 2006 (UIGEA) and Internet laws that might be passed in the future? The inclusion of these Internet laws could be problematic given ongoing disagreements within the U.S. Department of Justice over whether and what Internet gaming is legal under the Wire Act and given the ambiguous language within UIGEA. As to future enactments of Internet gaming laws, tribal nations should not be required to comply with changing federal laws without their consent or meaningful involvement in the drafting of these laws. Even more troubling is the requirement that each tribal nation ordinance must be accompanied by the previous three years of financial records of the tribal nation, information on all organizational and related businesses and affiliates of the tribal nation, and a waiver of sovereign immunity even if the tribal nation is not intending to operate the online gaming itself. These requirements are much more expansive and intrusive than IGRA now requires.

We must object to the peculiar provision in the Committee's draft bill that requires federal disapproval of a tribal nation's ordinance if the Secretary determines that the "tribal governing body was significantly and unduly influenced by any person in the adoption of the ordinance or resolution". Setting aside the odd nature of this standard, how exactly would the Secretary make such a determination? And in making such a determination, how would the Committee propose to guard against the Secretary him or herself being significantly and unduly influenced in making this determination? This is no specious concern, given the record of significant and undue influence upon the Congress itself in its consideration of online gaming legislation.

State Jurisdiction. Section 9 is objectionable because it permits any *State* regulatory body that regulates casino gaming to ask the Secretary to designate it as a tribal qualified body for purposes of regulating tribal online gaming, including the review of applications, the issuance of licenses and carrying out other regulatory and enforcement functions. This is completely unacceptable. Under current IGRA sanctioned tribal-state compacts very few states provide regulatory and enforcement services to tribal nations, and then, only with the express consent of the tribe involved in exchange for other bargained for terms and conditions. In the few states where a state does have a role, it is generally limited to a review of tribal decisions made by the tribal regulatory agency. This section could embolden some states to overreach in negotiations with a tribal nation.

State Standards. Section 9 also is problematic because it requires tribal regulations on minimum requirements to be substantially equivalent to a state's regulations. Gaming tribes, including the Seneca Nation, have a very strong history of regulatory administration and compliance. It would be expected that these tribal nations likely would designate their existing tribal regulatory bodies or agencies to apply as tribal qualified bodies under the Act. Very few, if any tribes would permit a state to be eligible for designation as a qualified tribal regulatory body under the Act. Thus this reference to state regulations is both unnecessary and offensive.

The revenue sharing section is worthwhile topic for discussion but it will require further refinement in several respects. It should be clarified whether the revenue will be shared with all non-gaming Indian tribes or just those tribes that have opted out. It also makes sense that revenue sharing be regionalized to benefit only those tribes within proximity of the gaming tribes. There needs to be some flexibility for the contributing tribes to decide the specific criteria for the uses set out in section 7. Consideration must be given to the fact that gaming tribes in a few States already contribute gaming revenue to a revenue sharing account to avoid duplicative requirements. And, some thought should be given to the whether it makes sense to limit the revenue sharing to non-gaming, small tribes (population under 3,000) located in remote, isolated areas without any economic development opportunities. This issue is not easily resolved and requires the thoughtful input and involvement of all the tribes, regardless of whether they offer gaming.

Gaming tribes already have in place social responsibility protections that include self-exclusion, compulsive gambling assistance and responsible gaming notices. Tribal nations with established programs should be allowed to grandfather their existing programs.

Ambiguous Terms. The draft legislation makes imprecise or inconsistent use of key terms such as "gambling," "gaming," "Internet gaming," "Internet poker," "online gaming," "tribal online gaming," "tribal governing body" and "tribal qualified body." Many key terms are not defined at all. We would hope that further revisions of the bill place greater emphasis on definition of key terms and consistent use of such concepts throughout.

Non-Indian Entities in Consortia. The discussion draft appears to allow unrestricted participation in tribal online gaming by non-Indian entities so long as they are a part of a "consortium" that includes a tribal nation. Here, we see a risk of non-Indian competitors using affiliations with tribal nations to gain entry into the field of online gaming, particularly if there is no other legislative avenue available, or if the avenues that are available are more burdensome from a regulatory or financial perspective. We believe this provision should be substantially revised to ensure that the Act cannot be used in a way that would facilitate unfair entry into the field of tribal online gaming by non-Indian gaming competitors.

Sovereign Immunity. Provisions of the Act appear to potentially impair the sovereign immunity of tribal nations, requiring a tribal nation to subject itself to the jurisdiction of the applicable courts of the United States and all applicable Federal laws relating to the operation of an Internet poker facility and associated activities. We object to any statutory abrogation of tribal nation immunity from suit.

Relation to the Compact and State Involvement. Section 12 of the discussion draft provides that "Nothing in this Act (1) alters, diminishes, or otherwise impacts any right or obligation existing under a tribal-State compact approved pursuant to IGRA; or (2) requires the renegotiation of a compact . . . ." What this means and who this is intended to benefit is ambiguous. Most tribal-state compacts limit the tribal nation to conducting only those Class III games specifically listed therein. The discussion draft provision could be interpreted to place a limitation on a tribal nation's ability to engage in online gaming, or at a minimum, create a compact dispute. We believe the discussion draft should be clarified to say that "tribal online gaming" does not require a compact with, or the consent of, any state.

Conclusion. For all of the foregoing reasons, the discussion draft must be substantially overhauled and revised, and that can only happen with the active and open participation of tribal nations and their representatives. Please let us know how we can join with you in rehabilitating this discussion draft.